Starting with Ducks

Katie Thear

STARTING WITH DUCKS

First published by Broad Leys Publishing Ltd: 2002.
Reprinted 2004 and 2005.

Copyright © 2002, 2004 and 2005. Katie Thear

Printed by Design and Print Ltd.

A catalogue record for this book is available from the British Library.

ISBN: 0 906137 30 6

Outside front cover: Whalesbury duck.

Outside back cover: Top: White Indian Runners.
                      Bottom: Mandarin drake.

Unless indicated otherwise all photographs were taken by the author.
The old drawings in this book have, in some cases, had the backgrounds removed for greater clarity and have been computer-enhanced by Broad Leys Publishing Ltd

For details of other publications please see Page 96.

Broad Leys Publishing Ltd
1 Tenterfields,
Newport, Saffron Walden,
Essex CB11 3UW, UK.

Tel/Fax: 01799 541065
E-mail: kdthear@btinternet.com
Website: www.blpbooks.co.uk

Contents

The author with some of her ducks. They are being given their afternoon grain feed.

Preface

Most people are fond of ducks. Who could possibly dislike them? Everyone has at some time enjoyed watching them, even if it is only in the public park.

This book is for those who wish to go a bit further - by keeping their own flock of ducks. The reasons for doing so are many. It may be for pure enjoyment or there may be a wish to keep particular breeds of domestic ducks. Some may want to supplement their winter eggs at a time when chickens tend to lay less, or there may be a wish to start a small table duck enterprise. Those with large ponds or lakes may wish to consider keeping ornamental ducks or provide conditions for visiting wildfowl. Whatever the aims, I hope that the information in this book will prove to be useful. If you wish to contact me for any additions or amendments for future editions, my address is at the beginning of the book, or my E-mail is katie@blpbooks.co.uk

The book is written for those who are considering keeping ducks for the first time, but I hope that experienced duck-keepers will also glean useful information from it. It is up-to-date and covers the relevant legislation.

Finally, I am grateful to the many people and organisations who have contributed their advice and information for this first edition. They are listed in the reference section at the end.

Katie Thear, Newport, 2002.

Introduction

I can honestly say that I know of no livestock which can prove of more interest or give so much pleasure.
(Reginald Appleyard)

Keeping any living creature is not without its problems and it would be wrong to imply otherwise. It is important to clarify the reasons for wanting to keep ducks, and to establish appropriate conditions for them. They are waterfowl and need access to water for swimming, dabbling or diving, as befits their nature. The water needs to be kept well aerated so that stagnant conditions are avoided, otherwise disease may result.

Ducks are at their best where they have room to roam and forage. Small gardens may only be suitable for a pair of bantam ducks which will cause less damage to lawns and flower beds, unless an aviary or enclosed enclosure is provided. Ducks generally leave messy droppings and a number of birds can soon produce a mudbath.

They need to be looked after every day of the year, including holidays, so arrangements will need to be made for their care and feeding in the event of any absence. Although they are generally hardy creatures and are not bothered by rain, they do dislike high winds. They need adequate housing and shelter, and must also be protected against predators. Ornamentals may also require extra frost protection.

It is a good idea to visit farm or wildfowl parks where a variety of breeds can be seen. Visiting agricultural or poultry shows where ducks are being shown is also worth doing, and provides an excellent opportunity to talk to breeders. There are also national and local societies that look after the interests of specific breeds.

DEFRA (Department of the Environment, Farming & Rural Affairs) has a free booklet *Codes of Recommendations for the Welfare of Livestock: Ducks*. This is essential reading for all duck-keepers. In it, five freedoms are specified:

• Freedom from thirst, hunger and malnutrition by ready access to fresh water and a diet to maintain full health and vigour.

• Freedom from discomfort by providing an appropriate environment including shelter and a comfortable resting area.

• Freedom from pain, injury, infestation or disease by prevention or by rapid diagnosis and treatment.

• Freedom to display normal patterns of behaviour.

• Freedom from fear and distress.

If these conditions are provided, the result will be contented ducks.

Ducks in History

Votive offering, 6000BC, photographed by the author at Delos Museum, Greece.

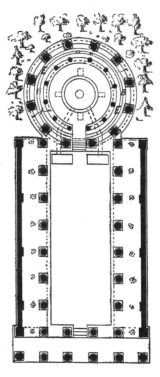

Duck motif in a section of Roman mosaic flooring photographed by the author at Merida, Spain.

Plan of the Bird-house at Casinum, as described by the Roman author Varro. It included an island and staging, as well as duck houses. *(Rerum Rusticarum, Varro, AD46)*

Ulissi Aldrovandi, the 16th century naturalist, claimed that ducks grew on trees. As the 'duck fruits' ripened, they fell into the water as ducklings! *(Historica Naturalis, 16th century).*

Decoy (call) ducks being used to lure wildfowl into a decoy or trapping net. *(The Decoy, Nolan, 1850)*

About the duck

Four ducks on a pond, a grass bank beyond.
(William Allingham, 1870)

Old style Aylesbury *(Harrison Weir, 19th century)*

Ducks were known to our prehistoric ancestors, judging by the bones found in caves such as Kirkdale in Yorkshire, Kent's cavern in Devon and Hoe Grange in Derbyshire. They would have been wild ducks, either resident in these islands or migratory species visiting on a seasonal basis. It is a matter of conjecture how the skilful hunters caught them, but they were evidently important in the diet.

Ducks were familiar to all the great civilisations of the past. Egyptian artefacts show wild ducks being netted in the Nile delta. Later dynasties there developed the art of artificial incubation, a practice that would almost certainly have led to some degree of selective breeding and hence domestication, although there is no other evidence to support this.

The Roman writer Varro, in his wonderful treatise *Rerum Rusticarum*, gives details of feeding and managing flocks of ducks, as well as including a plan of the bird house, island and ponds that were built in Casinum.

Origin of domestic breeds

All breeds of domestic ducks (with the exception of the Muscovy) are descended from strains of the wild Mallard, *Anas platyrhynchos*. The Muscovy, *Cairina moschata*, evolved in South America as a distinct species.

White strains of Mallard initially appeared as 'sports' or genetic mutations. These would have been more at risk in the wild, than their better camouflaged kin, so it is likely that they survived by taking up residence close to man. Once humans had settled in agricultural settlements, rather than being hunter-gatherers, they established colonies of various livestock around them. One assumes that these included semi-domesticated flocks of ducks.

In medieval times it was common for ducks, geese and chickens to be handed over as part of the rent due to the lord of the manor. In the 16th century, Tusser's advice, *"With doves good luck, reare goose and duck"*, also indicates their importance as farmed birds. In the 17th century, Markham recommends the use of, *"large pens of three feet high for geese, ducks and fowle"*.

In the 19th century, in the first edition of her *Book of Household Management*, Mrs Beeton has a lot to say about various breeds of ducks and their characteristics, but apparently does not approve of their feeding habits. *"It is excessively greedy and by no means a nice feeder"*, she states rather primly, although the duck's culinary

Wild Mallard, *Anas platyrhynchos*, the ancestor of all breeds of domestic duck.

The Muscovy, *Cairina moschata*, is related to the wild Musk or Brazilian duck of South America.

assets do seem to have had a softening effect on her: *"Its flesh is savoury, being not so gross as that of the goose."* Up until this time, ducks were primarily regarded as utility birds for the table, with egg production taking a secondary role.

Trapping ducks for food was, and is, an ancient activity. In 19th century England, Decoy or Call ducks were used to entice wildfowl down onto water and into trapping or decoy nets. (Nolan's picture on page 6 shows this). Call ducks came from the Netherlands where they had originally arrived from Asia, but they were first standardized in Britain. Originally called Coys or Decoys, their loud quacks were used to lure wildfowl down onto the water where they could be trapped. These days, wild fowlers in areas such as the Norfolk Broads are more likely to use wooden or plastic decoy ducks to float on the water, while they emulate duck calls with a purpose-made, blowing 'quacker'.

Ducks generally have been developed, over many generations, as table birds and egg layers, but an increasing number of people are now keeping them for showing, interest and certainly for pleasure.

Mallard male and female. Unlike domestic ducks (apart from small breeds and the Muscovy), they have not lost the ability to fly.
Gould's Birds of Britain (King Penguin series)

Classification

Before taking a more detailed look at specific breeds and their management, it is worth 'placing' ducks in the system of classification devised by Linnaeus in the 18th century, and seeing how they relate to the rest of the bird kingdom:

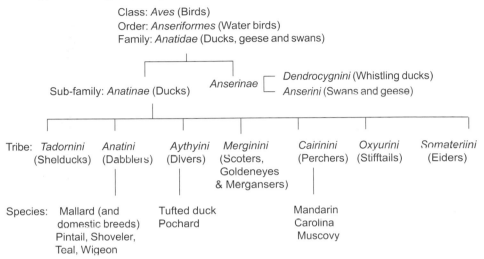

The table obviously does not show all the breeds of ducks, but it does indicate the relationship that exists between the various types. The species listed are some of the most commonly kept ones.

Types of duck

The ducks that are most commonly kept can be differentiated into three types: *diving* ducks, *dabblers* and *perching* ducks.

• **Diving breeds**, such as the Tufted duck and Pochard, can submerge to a considerable depth to obtain their food. This includes plants, insect larvae, crustaceans and small fish, as well as organisms that are likely to be disturbed by poking around in the mud at the bottom.

• **Dabbling ducks**, such as the Mallard and the domestic breeds, obtain their food on or near the surface. The fact that they are dabblers does not mean that they are unable to submerge, but merely that they have a greater tendency to dabble about on the surface. This is related to the fact that their diet is mainly gleaned from floating plants and the insect larvae and crustaceans that adhere to them. They frequently 'up-end' and dabble below the surface, leaving only the tail above water.

Perching ducks, such as the Mandarin and Carolina, are adapted to perching and nesting in trees, although they obviously do spend time on water. In the wild, they nest in tree-holes, but will use nest boxes that are provided for them. The Muscovy is also a percher, but is more like the goose in its tendency to graze on grassland.

Having a knowledge of the type of duck enables one to plan for appropriate conditions. Diving ducks, for example, will need deeper water than that provided for dabblers, while tree ducks such as the Mandarin will need nest boxes that are raised from the ground. Muscovy ducks will generally adapt well to using ground nest boxes, although straw bales to climb on and perch are appreciated. It is also possible to differentiate ducks into *domestic breeds*, *ornamental breeds* and *wildfowl*:

• **Domestic ducks** are breeds which are or have been kept for utility purposes on the farm or smallholding and which provide eggs or meat. Down feathers are also gleaned from domestic ducks, although the traditional source is the Eider duck.

There are breed standards for domestic ducks, which have been drawn up by the appropriate breed societies and national organisations. The aim is to provide an ideal standard to which breeders can aspire, so that their ducks are the best possible when compared with the ideal. This has produced a division within the domestic breeds into *show* breeds and *utility* strains. The former have an emphasis on the required standard of appearance, while the latter have more emphasis on their productive capacity. Utility birds have often been crossed or hybridized in order to make them more suitable for commercial purposes. Strains of Pekin and Aylesbury, for example, have been used to produce commercial table ducks.

In addition to the normal-sized domestic breeds there are *Bantam* or *Miniature* ducks, which as the names indicate are smaller in size. Call ducks are given the separate classification of *Calls*, although they are designated as *Bantams* in the USA.

• **Ornamental ducks** are those that are kept primarily for their appearance on ponds and lakes, but they are not domestic breeds or show birds. They include dabbling, diving and perching ducks, and are often seen in waterfowl collections and bird parks. The following are classified as ornamentals by the *British Waterfowl Association*: Mandarin, Carolina, and all other species of British or foreign wild ducks.

• **Wildfowl** is a general name given to wild waterfowl. It includes ducks, geese and swans. Many are migratory birds, coming to lakes on a seasonal basis. It is also a term that is frequently used as an alternative to *Ornamentals.*

Characteristics

All members of the *Anatinae* (Ducks) family have characteristics in common. They are generally small birds (by comparison with geese), and have relatively short legs and necks. They tend to walk rather clumsily on land but are well adapted for water and muddy areas at the sides of ponds and lakes.

The large, webbed feet are powerful paddles for swimming or squelching in the mud. Those of perching ducks have longer claws as an adaptation to their tree perching activities. The legs or shanks are protected by close-fitting and overlapping scales. These are *scutellate* or shield-shaped scales, rather than the *reticulate* or net-shaped ones found in geese and swans.

Ducks are well adapted to water and regard it as a security area away from predators, as well as a medium for providing food. These are wild ducks, the result of cross-breeding between farm ducks and wild Mallards.

The general shape, with the centre of gravity in the keel, as in a boat, enables a duck to maintain its balance in the water, and the highly mobile neck allows for sudden foraging movements if prey is sighted. Compared with the dabblers, the diving ducks tend to have shorter, rounder bodies, with feet set further back for more effective propulsion downwards through the water.

Generally speaking, the plumage of the male and females differ, with the drake being more colourful and resplendent than the female. The Mallard has passed on the genetic factor for curled tail feathers to the drakes of most of the domestic breeds, a factor that is useful for sexing young birds. The calls of the sexes are also different, with the females having a definite 'quack', while the drakes produce a less definite, half-quack. The Muscovy has no quack at all, confining itself to hisses and puffs.

The duck's body is kept warm by a thick inner layer of light down feathers, whose value in quilt-making has been appreciated for hundreds of years. The outer feathers are kept covered by oil from the bird's preen gland, which is situated just above the root of the tail. Water will literally 'run off a duck's back'.

The bill has nostrils and a rounded hook or 'bean' on the end, which helps the duck to catch hold of plants and prey in the water. Along the edges there are serrations called *lamellae* that strain the water so that food is retained. In diving ducks these are fewer but larger and more saw-like so that fish and other prey can be caught more easily. In the Shoveler, *Anas clypeata*, the bill is long and broad for efficient 'scooping up' of minute animal organisms and plants near the surface.

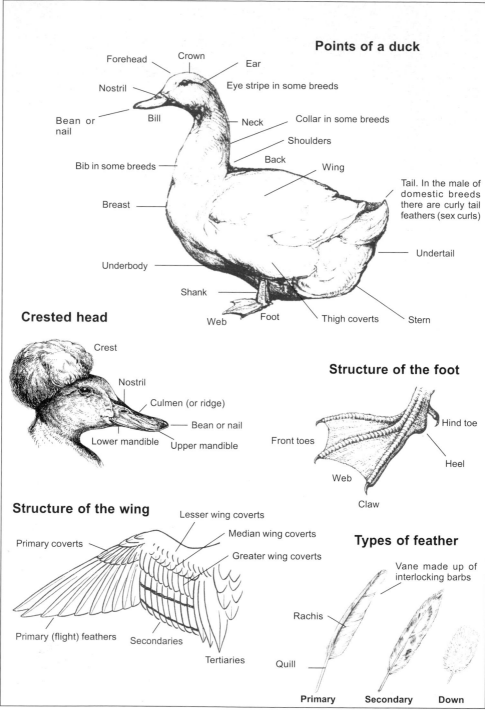

Points of a duck

Forehead
Crown
Ear
Eye stripe in some breeds
Nostril
Bean or nail
Bill
Neck
Collar in some breeds
Shoulders
Back
Wing
Bib in some breeds
Tail. In the male of domestic breeds there are curly tail feathers (sex curls)
Breast
Underbody
Undertail
Shank
Web
Foot
Thigh coverts
Stern

Crested head

Crest
Nostril
Culmen (or ridge)
Bean or nail
Lower mandible
Upper mandible

Structure of the foot

Hind toe
Front toes
Heel
Web
Claw

Structure of the wing

Lesser wing coverts
Median wing coverts
Greater wing coverts
Primary coverts
Primary (flight) feathers
Secondaries
Tertiaries

Types of feather

Vane made up of interlocking barbs
Rachis
Quill
Primary
Secondary
Down

The drakes of most of the domestic breeds have inherited the curly tail feathers (sex curls) of their ancestor the wild Mallard.

Moulting

Most ducklings are fully feathered by the age of six weeks. The juvenile plumage is then retained until late summer to autumn when there is a moult of the body feathers, to be replaced by the adult ones. However, the wing feathers are retained until the following late summer, when there is a complete moult.

There are exceptions to this pattern, of course. The Gadwalls, Shoveler and Teal, for example, take longer to make the transition from juvenile to adult plumage, taking most of the autumn and winter to achieve this. Others, such as the Mandarin, Carolina, diving ducks and Pintails are usually in full plumage colour by December.

All birds moult, in that feathers are dropped to be replaced by new ones, but the males of the *Anatinae* family have a double moult. The first is the *nuptial moult* after which the colourful mating plumage appears. This is retained until summer to autumn. After this, the second or *eclipse moult* takes place. This is where more drab plumage, like that of the females, provides camouflage at a time when the loss of primary and secondary feathers make flight impossible. It is normally a short period of about two months before the brightly coloured nuptial feathers are grown again.

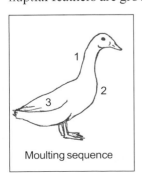

Moulting sequence

The Mallard, Muscovy, ornamentals and Calls have retained the ability to fly. To stop them flying away, they may need to be kept in enclosures or have the wing feathers trimmed. (See page 54 for further details of wing clipping and pinioning).

Muscovy losing neck and wing feathers in the annual moult.

A children's rigid plastic paddling pool adapted to provide a pond for the ducks. It is light and easy to empty and refill. Here it is in use at an agricultural show display.

A newly-made pond of heavy duty butyl rubber sheeting. The wooden planks and random flagstones are holding down the edges until a more permanent edging of flagstones can be supplied. Meanwhile, the birds are already happy to use the facilities. *(H.D. Sharman)*

Access to water

Ceiliog bach y Wyddfa yn canu ar y bryn,
Hwyaid Aberglaslyn yn nofio ar y llyn.

Snowdon's little cockerel singing on the hill,
Aberglaslyn's ducks swimming on the lake.
(Traditional Welsh)

(Harrison Weir, 1890)

Waterfowl would hardly be called as such unless they had a requirement for this medium in their environment. Dabbling ducks need to be able to swim about, ducking their heads under water and generally making use of the medium in a way that their natures demand. Diving ducks obviously need deep water and are only appropriate to those with deeper ponds or lakes on their land. Perching ducks are more land-based but still need access to water. Our Muscovy ducks always preferred the company of the geese and spent much of their time in the field, but from time to time, they also enjoyed a dip in the pond.

It is often forgotten that having access to water also represents security for ducks. Many a duck has escaped the attentions of a fox because there was a pond nearby. Ours were never taken by foxes, although we did have some chicken losses. In the case of wildfowl, an island retreat in the middle of a lake is common. An artificial island can be created by making a wooden raft with empty plastic bottles attached underneath to provide bouyancy. The whole thing is then anchored in the pond.

The volume of water available to ducks will obviously depend upon individual sites and circumstances. There are many options available, but the salient points when making a pond, are that it should be away from overhanging trees that would shed leaves into it, and that there is sufficient aeration to avoid stagnant conditions.

Botulism organisms thrive in the anaerobic (without air) conditions of a stagnant pond, but cannot do so if the water is clean and well aerated. The larger the pond, the greater the surface area for atmospheric oxygen to diffuse into the water, and for carbon dioxide to be released back into the air.

Large stretches of water represent a complete eco-system, with submerged, floating, marginal plants and microscopic phyto-plankton also taking in carbon dioxide for photosynthesis and producing oxygen as a waste product. Crustaceans, insect larvae, fish and amphibians also benefit from the plants, using them as food and shelter, as well as an oxygen source. Ducks in such an environment, add to and benefit from the food and oxygen chains. Their movements stir up the water, thereby increasing the aeration, their droppings add to the fertility and nutrient requirements of the plants and smaller life forms, and they keep a balance within the eco-system by eating a proportion of them. The Chinese, who developed the Pekin duck, have a long tradition of using water, ducks and fish in such a balanced environment.

If a hosepipe connection is used with an outside tap, it is necessary to have a valve to prevent the backflow of water so that water regulations are complied with.

A farm pump with a stone trough that can be refilled for the provision of clean water.

Water is a great draw. Older children are usually safe, but it may be necessary to net a pond if there are toddlers or young children in the vicinity. It is still possible to make an access point for the ducks.

Volume and depth requirements

It is difficult to be precise about the duck's needs in relation to water, for little research has been done into the subject. How deep should the water be? What area of water is required for a given number? As referred to earlier, different types of ducks have different needs, while the level of aeration is also a factor. The following comments are based on my own observations and are general recommendations only. They should not be regarded as definitive.

• If dabbling ducks are to be able to dabble and up-end effectively, the depth of water needs to be at least 30cm (12in). To be able to surface swim and dip their heads, the depth needs to be at least 15cm (6in).

• For divers to be able to dive effectively, the depth should be at least 90cm (3ft)

• To avoid water freezing solid in hard winters, the minimum depth should be 90cm (3ft)

• To provide the maximum sense of security for all ducks, the minimum depth should be at least 90cm (3ft)

• In relatively still water, the density should not exceed 4 ducks per 1sq.m (10sq.ft)

• In flowing water, the density should not exceed 8 ducks per 1 sq.m (10sq.ft)

• If it is only possible to provide ducks with water of a sufficient depth to submerge the head only, no diving ducks should be kept.

Providing water

There are several options when it comes to providing water, depending on the amount of land, number and type of ducks, and the size and scale of the enterprise.

Paddling pool

This is one of the easiest and cheapest ways of providing a pool for a small number of ducks. I first saw the rigid plastic one illustrated on page 14 at a smallholding show, and thought what a good idea it was, particularly for emergency use. The owner had removed the original clam cover and fixed a metal gauge ramp where the hinges had been. I subsequently enquired at several toy shops and found that this type of paddling pool is widely available.

Inflatable rubber paddling pools can also be used, but are not as robust as the rigid plastic type, although they are easier to empty.

It is obviously necessary to refill the pool regularly, and tipping it up is not always easy. An old-fashioned stirrup pump is ideal, if you can find one. Alternatively, a large siphon of the type that you squeeze to get it going, is useful.

On an even smaller scale, a plastic baby-bath with brick or flagstone supports around it, and a plank ramp going up to it, will keep a pair of small ducks happy.

Purpose-made ponds for dabbling ducks

A *Sycon* duck pool photographed at a show.

Domestic Fowl Trust's duck pond with ball valve

Adapting an old sink

Old sinks are not as common as they were, now that gardeners use them for making miniature gardens or patio containers. Where one is available, it can be converted into a small pond for a couple of small ducks, by placing it over a soak-away. The latter is made by digging a hole at least 60cm (2ft) deep and around 15cm (6in) wider all round than the sink. The hole is then filled with hardcore topped with gravel. Depending on the depth of the sink, it can either be sunk into the gravel or rest on top of it. If the latter is the case, and it is a deep sink, it will be necessary to provide a ramp. Once the plug is in position, the sink can be filled and is ready for use. When it needs emptying, it is simply a matter of removing the plug and allowing the water to drain away into the soak-away. From here, it gradually disperses, without causing marshy conditions.

Bear in mind that where a hosepipe is used, there is a by-law requirement for an outside tap to be fitted with a valve that prevents back-flow.

Purpose-made duck ponds

Some poultry equipment suppliers sell purpose-made duck ponds which can easily be incorporated into a run or enclosure. They are fairly shallow and not suitable for divers. They often come with ramps, as well as in-flow and out-flow pipes. Some have feeders incorporated as optional extras.

Concrete ponds

These were popular at one time, but in recent years have been superseded by pond liners, unless there is specific need for a raised pond such as that for koi fish, or for diving breeds. They are certainly strong but are labour-intensive to construct.

Ideally, a pond should be constructed with a slight slope so that a drain facility with filter can be installed at the lower end. It is important to stress that a draining facility should not affect any neighbouring property.

A hole is dug to size, allowing for a total concrete in-fill of 15cm (6in) depth. The sides are sloped to an angle of around 45 degrees and the soil tamped down. The hole

Here a waterfall is providing excellent aeration for a small lake used by ornamental ducks. Note the island platform for the birds and the sitting/viewing area for people.

is then lined with polythene sheeting and concreted to an initial depth of 10cm (4in). Sections of wire netting can be pressed into the concreted sides to reinforce them. A final 5cm (2in) layer of concrete is then applied and smoothed. When dry, a proprietary sealant is painted on. Once this is completely dry, the pond can be filled. Concreting needs to be done when there is no danger of frost, and if it is done over a period of several days, it should be kept covered up.

Pond liners

The quickest and most convenient way of making a pond is by using a pond liner. They are available in rigid or flexible forms. The rigid, or pre-formed type, are made of plastic or fibreglass. The latter is stronger and more durable, but both are more suitable for small, shallow ponds.

The best pond liner, in my view, is the butyl or synthetic rubber sheeting. It is flexible, adaptable and will stretch. It can be used for large, deep ponds, and is also durable, with a life of many years. Heavy duty butyl is less likely to puncture than other liners. There are cheaper, PVC liners but they are thinner and likely to tear.

Whatever type of sheeting is used, the hole is first marked out and excavated to the appropriate size and depth. A 30cm (12in) wide shelf of around the same depth can be included in the excavation so that marginal plants can be planted. (These will need to be protected with some wire mesh until they are well-established). The hole is lined with sand and the flexible liner is then laid across, making sure that it is centrally placed, with a few supporting stones around the edges. A sunny day with no wind is

Minimum depths of water and maximum flock densities

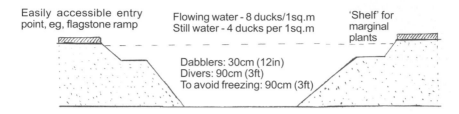

Easily accessible entry point, eg, flagstone ramp

Flowing water - 8 ducks/1sq.m
Still water - 4 ducks per 1sq.m

'Shelf' for marginal plants

Dabblers: 30cm (12in)
Divers: 90cm (3ft)
To avoid freezing: 90cm (3ft)

the ideal time to do this, for the sun warms up the liner and makes it more flexible. Gradually fill the pond and the liner will stretch and take up its position in the hole. (Move the stones as necessary to allow for this). Once the pond is full, fold and trim the liner, allowing a generous overlap around the bank. Place flagstones around the bank to hide and reinforce the liner.

Traditional puddled clay pond

The traditional way of making a pond was to 'puddle' it. This involved laying down a thick layer of clay and tamping or stamping it into place. This was the method used for making the network of canals in the 19th century. (The canal builders used to drive herds of cattle along the newly-clayed sections of canal so that the cattle hooves did the puddling). This method obviously works best where the soil is naturally heavy and where there is an existing low-lying, marshy area. It is possible to buy in loads of clay but it is expensive. These days, a heavy-duty butyl liner is the preferred option.

Restoring an old farm pond

Many people claim that it is not possible to have fish, plants and ducks, all living in harmony in a pond. We proved them wrong as far as our pond was concerned. It appeared on old maps of the area, but was so stagnant that the only sign of life (if one could call it that) was the occasional bubble of methane that surfaced.

On a particularly dry summer, when the level had fallen quite low, we began to clear it. The amount of smelly, decayed matter that we removed was enormous, but proved to be a valuable addition to the compost when sandwiched between straw. By the time we had finished, the depth in the centre was around 150cm (5ft) and we cut a new 'shelf' all around in order to plant marginals. We also made an easy 'ramp' access for ducks. We reasoned that they would tend to use this so the planted side areas would be less likely to be damaged, and so it proved. Even so, the plants were given protective 'tents' of wire netting until they were established. They looked strange for a couple of months, but the technique worked and once the netting was removed, the plants not only survived but thrived. The marginal plants that we introduced were Marsh Marigold (King Cup), *Caltha palustris*, and Bogbean, *Menyanthes trifoliata*. In the deeper part we planted a couple of Water Lilies, *Nymphaea alba*. The central,

The author's pond before and after restoration

Before being cleared, the pond was stagnant, smelly and lifeless.

After being cleared and planted with marginals, it became the home of fish, amphibians and ducks.

Some of the author's ducks feeding on the aptly-named Duckweed. It proved to be one of the most important elements in their diet and arguably diverted their attention from the marginal plants.

deep area was kept clear, but we introduced some weighted bunches of Canadian pondweed, *Elodea canadensis,* as oxygenating plants in the shallower parts. The tiny floating plants Common Duckweed, *Lemna minor*, appeared on their own, probably caught on the feet of visiting wild ducks. It is a well-named plant and proved to be immensely popular with our ducks. They spent hours 'grazing', an activity that argu-ably diverted their attention from the decorative marginal plants.

Before we refilled the pond, we made some 'fish shelters'. These were a few bricks with flagstones on top, placed on the bottom of the pond. We reasoned that if we provided such safe havens for the fish, only the slowest would be caught, and so it proved. We did not introduce fish until the following spring. They included ordinary Goldfish, Golden Orfe, a couple of Green Tench and some Catfish as bottom feeders. Frogs, toads and newts appeared of their own accord, and while there must have been losses to the ducks, there was also a balance, for every spring we had mounds of frog spawn and strings of toad spawn. In fact, it was visiting herons after the fish which proved to be the greatest nuisance, but that is another story.

Refilling the pond with a hosepipe, once it had been cleared and prepared took the best part of two days. At first, it looked like mud soup and our hearts sank, but after a couple of days, it was unbelievably clear. It did not remain so, of course, for like most pond owners, we soon discovered the bugbear of green algae. Then we discovered how effective the use of barley straw is as a control method. If some is placed in a net bag and immersed in the pond in winter, the toxins that are then gradually released have an inhibiting effect on the algae, without affecting the ducks, fish or amphibians. There are also proprietary products such as *Aquaplankton* available.

Here, an existing stream has been 'partitioned' so that different breeds have their own section. In this way there is no risk of inter-breeding. The sides of the upper stream have been reinforced with logs.

Using an existing stream

The best way of all of providing water, without the need for emptying, refilling, aerating and so on, is to use an existing stream. If you have one running across your land, you are indeed fortunate. The simplest way of using it is to partition it so that different breeds have their own sections, without being able to cross from one area to the next. This prevents inter-breeding, an important aspect for those who are concentrating on this aspect of duck-keeping. It is often called the Dutch system and there are many variations of it. On a large scale, it was used at the beginning of the 20th century, to raise Pekin table birds on Long Island, New York. In some areas of the world, this system is still used for table ducks (See page 44) and ensures that ducks are provided with reasonably natural conditions, rather than the intensive houses that are normally used.

If a small dam is constructed to make a pool, it is important to have adequate facilities to allow the water to continue its course, via a leat. This is an outflow controlling the water flow so that while the pond is kept filled, the stream is essentially unabated. It also ensures that in the event of heavy rain and an increased torrent, the dam is not broken or the surrounding land flooded.

It may be necessary to reinforce the banks of a pond or stream. Dabbling ducks often erode the sides with their bills. Logs are often used, but a product called *Nicospan* has proved to be very popular and effective. (See page 26).

If water from a stream is dammed or diverted in any way, it is necessary to obtain permission from the Environment Agency.

A large duck farm on Long Island, New York, with pens extending down into the tidal water. (*USDA Bulletin* - Duck Raising. 1915)

Pumps

A pump can be used to provide movement in water or to power an aerating fountain, if necessary. There are basically two types of pump: a *mains surface* or a *low-voltage submersible*. The former is an expensive option, requiring a qualified electrician to install it. It is usually housed in a pump chamber that is clear of the pond and is more applicable to larger ponds than small ones.

Low-voltage submersible pumps are widely available in garden centres and are put in the pond, on a platform above the silt layer. They are a cheap option and will effectively power a small fountain. This is enough to aerate the pond, but will not remove any detritus from the water. For this to happen, there must either be a filter or the water must be removed and replenished.

A low-voltage pump is connected by low-voltage, heavy duty cable to the mains via a transformer; this steps down the mains current to 12v or 24v. The lead from the pump is connected to the low voltage cable from the mains with a waterproof connector on land. It is a good idea to run it through a plastic conduit pipe, then bury it and place it under a flagstone where it is protected but accessible.

Recent introductions are solar-powered pumps. These are of two kinds: a *ground-placed solar panel* and a *floating unit*. The first is where a small solar panel is placed on the ground near to the pond, with the appropriate wiring going to the pump which is in the pond. The second is a complete unit that floats in the water. When the sun shines on it, it automatically sets a small fountain going. Once installed, solar powered pumps are the cheapest to run but they will obviously only function when there is sufficient sunlight available.

Here, a stream has been dammed to provide a pool. The water is still able to flow through a leat so that, in the event of an increased torrent, flooding is avoided.

Having a netting barrier across a stream effectively keeps ducks within their own area.

A low-powered submersible pump operating a fountain for aeration

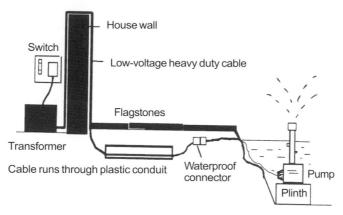

- Switch
- House wall
- Low-voltage heavy duty cable
- Flagstones
- Transformer
- Cable runs through plastic conduit
- Waterproof connector
- Pump
- Plinth

Pond overflow

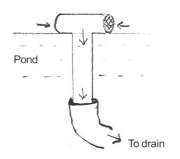

- Pond
- To drain

Ramp access to a pond

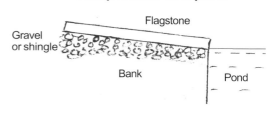

- Flagstone
- Gravel or shingle
- Bank
- Pond

Reinforcing a bank with Nicospan

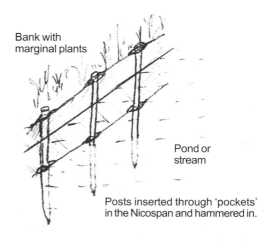

- Bank with marginal plants
- Pond or stream
- Posts inserted through 'pockets' in the Nicospan and hammered in.

A floating solar panel powered fountain to provide aeration of water, but only while the sun is shining.

Housing

There are features that make some houses more suitable than others. A duck is a waterfowl, strong and clever in its natural element, but awkward on land. (Will Hooley)

(Harrison Weir, 1897)

When it comes to housing, the needs of ducks are straightforward. Whatever the scale, a house needs to provide a dry floor, a waterproof roof, shelter from the wind and good ventilation. A poultry house can be used, as long as the perches are removed. As ducks emerge in a tightly packed waddle, it is no good relying on a chicken pop-hole. The door itself will need to be opened so that there is a wide exit. If this is off the ground, a wide ramp will be needed. If necessary, a door can be rehung so that it opens downwards and outwards, providing a ramp as it does so. The house should be positioned where the door opens away from prevailing winds.

Chicken house nest boxes are not suitable for ducks for they are generally too high. Laying ducks are more likely to use those that are low down and allow easy access. A narrow strip of wood retains the nesting material, without presenting a high obstacle. Wood shavings or chopped straw can be used as a nesting material, as well as on the floor of the house. Here it will provide a warm resting area but does tend to encourage floor-laid eggs. Domestic ducks have a habit of laying their eggs any-where, but providing suitable nesting areas is a positive encouragement. Some of my ducks used nest boxes while others ignored them. The nesting material and floor litter need to be changed regularly in order to keep the eggs and the general habitat clean.

As far as space within the house is concerned, large breeds need a minimum of 0.19sq.m (2sq.ft) of floor space per bird. Commercially, stocking density is worked out according to the weight of the birds in relation to the floor space. The RSPCA, for example, offers the following advice in its welfare standards for domestic ducks:

3 - 3.3kg	6 birds per 1sq.m
3.4 - 4.0kg	5 birds per 1sq.m

Ventilation can be provided above the birds' heads by a metal grille, slats or small holes bored through the wall, depending on the size and nature of the house.

The floor may be solid or slatted, but should be rat-proof. The roof should slope in such a way that rainwater is shed away from the door in order to prevent muddy conditions around the house.

On a small scale, movable houses are common. The simplest is probably an A-shaped structure that is boarded on three sides, with the open end being closed off by a metal grille door for night time security and ventilation. If there is no floor, it can be rested on a metal weldmesh panel on the ground. Straw placed on the panel then provides a comfortable resting area. On a larger scale, where laying or table ducks

Examples of duck housing

Here, a small house with drop-down ramp/door is used in one of several partitioned runs that have a stream running through them.

Dwyfor house on skids for ease of moving. It has a wide ventilation panel at the top. *(Gardencraft)*

House with solid floor and roof ridge ventilation. The door opens to form a ramp. *(Brakenfold)*

Lenham 705 house for 10-12 medium ducks, with ridge ventilation and removable side walls for cleaning. *(Forsham Cottage Arks)*

Lodge duck house with wide pop-hole, door and ventilation panel. *(Smiths Sectional Buildings)*

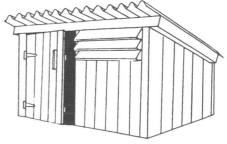

House for 8-10 ducks, with solid floor, sliding roof and louvre vents . *(Domestic Fowl Trust)*

These Muscovy ducks find the Dutch barn to their liking. It is well ventilated yet provides wind shelter and, if necessary, a perching area on the straw bales

are being reared, static houses and barns are commonly used. These usually have roof ridge ventilation as well as side vents. The floors are solid, with chopped straw or wood shavings litter, while wide doors allow ease of entrance and exit.

Aviary housing

The needs of ornamental ducks vary. They all need a secure enclosure from predators such as foxes, but as they are capable of flight, they are frequently kept in an aviary or covered enclosure, unless they have had one wing clipped or pinioned. (See page 54). Where they are kept free-winged, it is important to have an aviary that is high enough to allow them to fly around. Equally important is a double-door to prevent escapes.

Non-indigenous breeds are not as hardy as the northern, native breeds and may suffer frost damage to their feet unless they are protected. A house or aviary with a protected run is recommended for them. There are a number of suppliers of aviary buildings with covered runs, providing a range of different styles and sizes.

Equally important are the provisions of shade in summer and wind protection at all times, as well as a habitat where nest laying can take place. Strategically placed hurdles, straw bales or woven netting are effective in screening shelter areas, but plants such as reeds, shrubs and trees also provide a more natural habitat. Details of suitable plants are given on page 57.

The nesting requirements of ornamentals can vary quite considerably. Some breeds such as the Common Teal and Common Shoveler, are ground layers, while others such as the European Shelduck like partly underground nests with a tunnel entrance. Some, such as the Mandarin, lay their eggs in hollow trees or raised nest boxes. Further information on specific nesting sites and nest boxes is given on page 56 and in the table on pages 58-59.

Examples of anti-fox perimeter fencing

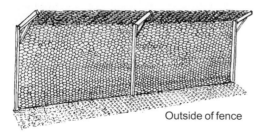

Outside of fence

A 2m (6.5ft) high perimeter fence with an extra 30cm (12in) overhang to deter climbing over. The netting is well dug in to prevent burrowing under.

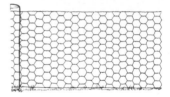

Poultry netting with 50mm holes is suitable, as long as it is supported by well-braced posts and is well tensioned to prevent sagging.

Elements of a small enclosure

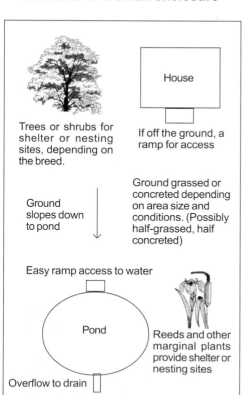

Trees or shrubs for shelter or nesting sites, depending on the breed.

House

If off the ground, a ramp for access

Ground slopes down to pond

Ground grassed or concreted depending on area size and conditions. (Possibly half-grassed, half concreted)

Easy ramp access to water

Pond

Reeds and other marginal plants provide shelter or nesting sites

Overflow to drain

Perimeter fence or covered enclosure to keep out predators and confine birds

Electric fencing

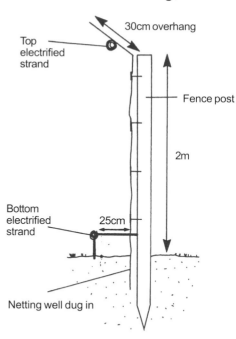

30cm overhang

Top electrified strand

Fence post

2m

Bottom electrified strand

25cm

Netting well dug in

Here, the perimeter fence is shown with added electric fencing. In this case, the fence does not need to be this high, as long as there are two electrified wires in front of it.

Ducks are vulnerable to predators, especially foxes, so it is necessary to ensure that they are safe from them. Ducks that have access to a large, deep pond or lake with an island are obviously safer, but it is still necessary to take precautions to ensure their safety. Most domestic ducks are unable to fly. Ornamentals that have been pinioned to prevent their flying away, or that are in eclipse moult, are also at risk. Domestic ducks and small, pinioned ornamentals are easy to confine so they require only a low barrier. A height of 60cm (2ft) is normally adequate. Thick hedges, stone walls, wooden fencing or poultry netting are all suitable, but these are for keeping ducks *in* rather than the fox *out*! Perching ducks that are good at climbing obviously need higher fencing. Any trees should well clear of the perimeter so that launch sites over the protective, boundary fence are not provided.

To exclude foxes from a site, it is necessary to have either high perimeter fences or ones that are reinforced with electric fencing. A height of at least 2m (6.5ft) is needed to keep out most foxes. A really determined one can even scale this height, so an added 30cm (12in) overhang is recommended, as shown in the diagram. The netting should also be well dug in to prevent burrowing under. Chain link fencing is ideal but it is also expensive. A cheaper alternative is to use ordinary poultry netting with 50mm holes, along post and rail fencing. The supporting posts need to be well dug in and braced, while the netting should be adequately tensioned to prevent sagging.

Within an enclosure, the conditions will vary, depending on the types of duck, but all ducks benefit from having well-drained ground that slopes down gently to the water. Grazers such as Muscovy and Wigeon need grass pasture. This may need to be mown periodically so that new, fresh growth is provided, rather than rank, coarse stems. Regular mowing or strimming is also important where electric fencing is used, otherwise 'shorting' of the current may occur.

If an area is to be sown for grazing, a poultry grass mixture that is made up of shorter perennial species is recommended. Specialist suppliers sell them and around 50g per 1 sq.m or 500kg per hectare, of seed will be needed.

As far as flock density outside is concerned, the following requirements are recommended by the RSPCA in their welfare standards for commercial ducks:

• Maximum of 4,000 ducks per hectare (1 duck per 2.5sq.m) where rotation ensures a good grass sward throughout the grass period.

• Maximum of 2,500 ducks per hectare (1 duck per 4sq.m) where grass is poor.

On a small or garden scale, these densities will vary depending on the site conditions and the types of ducks. It is up to the individual to ensure that adequate conditions are provided. It may be better, for example, to have a concrete run that is easily hosed down, rather than muddy terrain that harbours disease. Rotation of the pasture or land area is important in the prevention of disease and parasitic infestation. The fallow or 'resting' period of ground ensures that the life cycle of internal parasites is broken. It also allows time for the pasture to recover. Land left fallow can also be limed to 'sweeten' the ground and help to deal with residual parasites.

Pests and Predators

Reference has already been made to the necessity of protecting ducks against the fox, but there are other predators and pests that also pose a threat. While the fox is the most common, uncontrolled dogs can also be a nuisance. Again, high fences or electric fencing around the perimeters of the site will exclude them. Every flock owner has an individual responsibility to afford protection to the birds and these two measures are the only really effective ones. (See the diagrams on page 30).

Humane fox traps are available. These are large, baited cages that the animal enters and cannot get out of again. The trap needs to be placed on a pathway known to be frequented by the fox. It also needs to be well camouflaged for the fox is highly intelligent. If it is caught, there is still the problem of what to do with the captured animal. The most humane method of despatching it in this case, is with a 12 bore shotgun, as long as the owner holds a valid firearms certificate. There are those offering humane trapping and despatching services in most rural areas.

A flashing light can be a deterrent, as long as it is moved fairly frequently. Such units are available for use with electric fencing, or they can be incorporated into a normal fence. Chemical deterrents are available that act as a repellent when used along boundaries. *Renardine,* for example, can be mixed with sand and strewn along the perimeter. The treatment needs to be renewed weekly or after heavy rain. A family dog may keep a fox or strange dog away, while lion or tiger dung from the zoo placed along boundaries is also said to be effective. Llama owners are united in the belief that llamas will drive off foxes, but I have no personal experience of this.

Feral cats can sometimes pose a threat, particularly to young birds, but having one's own cat or family dog protecting their territories, is usually effective. It is worth remembering that while dog owners are responsible in law for keeping their dogs out of other people's property, the cat is recognised as having 'a natural propensity to roam', so it is up to the duck owner to keep the birds confined and the cat out.

Rats are a major pest because they are so numerous, prey on young birds, carry disease and cause considerable damage. If there is evidence that rats have been around, it is important to wash hands after touching any surfaces where their saliva, urine or droppings may have been deposited for they can transmit Weil's disease which can be fatal to humans. If ducks are showing a reluctance to go into a house or barn, where they have previously gone in without a fuss, suspect the presence of rats. Remove all the floor litter and check for holes at ground level. There is a statutory obligation to keep a site free of rats, either by reporting their presence to the local authority, or dealing with them yourself. A private householder will have the services of the pest control officer free of charge, but commercial sites must pay.

The average foraging distance of a rat is 50 metres, and if one rat is seen, you can be certain that there is a colony nearby. They tend to follow definite 'runs' so identifying these is the first priority. It is a good idea to cut down tall weeds growing against buildings and clearing areas where piles of timber or flagstones may have been left for some time. They often conceal rat runs. Inside outbuildings, paint a white strip along the floor perimeter to show up the presence of droppings more easily. The spindle-shaped droppings are quite large; up to 2cm long. Look for evidence of gnawing and block up any holes. All feeds should be stored in a rat-proof building or in a strong container with a tight-fitting lid. Dustbins, both metal and heavy-duty plastic, are ideal for this.

It is important not to leave food lying around to attract vermin. Self-operating feeders can be used where raiding rats or wild birds are feeding at your expense. These are feeders that dispense a certain amount of food to the ground when a lever or pedal is displaced by the duck, but which cannot be moved by lighter vermin.

Fenn traps are available for killing rats, but placing them is a skilled job, ensuring that they are in the runs, placed in tunnels and not accessible to anything else. As they are spring traps they need to be inspected regularly. There are also humane rat traps but again, there is the question of disposal of the live catch.

Poisoning is the most common option when it comes to rats. The bait needs to be placed carefully so that it is out of reach of wild birds, family pets and, of course, children. The main rodenticide used is an anti-coagulant such as that produced by *Sorex*. The baits are based on cereals and are available loose, in sachets or in blocks. The general rule is that if all the bait is taken on the first setting, double the amount placed the second time, and so on. This ensures that all the rats are being dealt with. It is a good idea to keep domestic cats confined until this operation is complete, for cases of poisoning as a result of catching the poisoned rats have been known.

Mice can be a nuisance in feed stores. Traps, both snap-on and live-catch are available, or sachets of poison similar to those available for rats can be placed in the appropriate areas. Mink, weasels and stoats can be a problem. The best approach is to fence them out, but this can be a problem because they can get in through relatively small apertures. A smooth fence, such as galvanised sheeting is effective because they cannot get a grip on the surface, but it is unsightly. Trapping is often used where mink are concerned, and special traps are available for them. Weasels and stoats, however, are indigenous species which are protected and should not be trapped. They can be deterred with a proprietary repellent, as referred to earlier, or soaking rags in diesel oil and hanging them around the perimeter has also been known to work.

Corvids such as rooks and magpies often steal eggs and can be a danger to fledglings. Larsen traps are frequently used for magpies, but as they are live-catch in case other, protected wild birds are caught, they must be inspected frequently. Both corvids and predatory hawks can be deterred by mirrors that reflect upwards, as well as by the use of scarecrows. There are also purpose-made raptor deterrents available from specialist suppliers. Again, birds of prey are protected species and must not be trapped. Finally, it is worth remembering that one of the worst predators can be the human thief, particularly where rare breeds or table-ready ducks are concerned. Lock them up securely!

Breeds

Miss Croad's imported Pekin drake.
(Harrison Weir, 1902)

There were three fat ducks that once I knew,
Fat ducks and pretty ones they were too.
But he with the feather curled up on his back,
Oh he was the fattest one! Quack, quack, quack.
(Traditional song)

Choosing the right breed for available conditions is an obvious priority. The choice is between domestic and ornamental breeds, but there are other sub-divisions and factors that are also relevant.

Domestic breeds

These, apart from the Muscovy, are dabblers that are all descended from the wild Mallard, so they share similar characteristics. They are utility birds in that they were originally developed for their productive capacity. Domestic breeds are classified by the British Waterfowl Association as *heavy*, *light*, *bantam* or *call* breeds. The first two include table and egg laying breeds respectively, while bantams and calls are kept mainly for pleasure and showing. In America, ducks have four classes: *heavy, medium, light* and *bantam*. For a detailed description of the standards, consult the appropriate publications: *British Waterfowl Standards* published by the BWA. (These standards also appear in *British Poultry Standards* published by Blackwell); *American Standard of Perfection* published by the American Poultry Association.

Heavy breeds

Ducks were originally kept and selected for their meat qualities, with eggs being regarded as a secondary consideration until the nineteenth century when a greater emphasis was placed on this factor. Heavy breeds usually weigh over 3.2kg (7lb) in females and over 3.6kg (8lb) in drakes.

Aylesbury

Aylesbury duck.
(Harrison Weir, 1891).

(See page 37). In 18th century England, the white-feathered strains of Mallard were initially called the White English duck. By the early nineteenth century, the area around Aylesbury became increasingly recognised as a market centre for quality, white-skinned, pinkish-billed table ducks. These were soon known as Aylesbury ducks, a breed that was also synonymous with large size and a horizontal carriage. In 1845 they were exhibited at the first British poultry show in a class for '*Aylesbury or other white variety*'. From Britain, they were exported all over the world. In the USA, however, yellow-skinned ducks were more popular commercially, and it was the Pekin that was to become the prime table bird. In

Above: Prize Aylesbury duck belonging to Mr John Gillies. *(Harrison Weir, 1902)*

Left: Pair of Aylesbury ducks belonging to Mrs Mary Seamons. *(Ludlow. 1874)*

1849, the Aylesbury was exhibited at the first American poultry show in Boston. The breed was included in the *American Standard of Perfection* in 1874.

Today's standards require the carriage to be horizontal with the keel parallel with the ground. The legs are strong to support the body, while the breast is well developed. Easy access to water and other areas is essential, particularly for mating, for the size and stance of the breed makes land mating difficult. Weights are 4.6 to 5.5kg (10-12lb) for the drake and 4.1 to 5kg (9-11lb) for the females.

The plumage is pure white and silky in both sexes, the bill is broad and long, pinkish white or flesh coloured, while the legs and feet are orange. The eyes are blue. Aylesbury ducks have a greater tendency towards broodiness than other breeds but are not good layers. The laying season is fairly short, normally extending from February to June until the annual moult. Average production is around 40 white to greenish eggs with good strains laying up to 100.

Many Aylesbury strains have had Pekin blood incorporated, so that size and carriage differ from the standard. The British Waterfowl Association has a campaign to save the exhibition Aylesbury because the numbers have declined in recent years.

Pekin

(See Page 37). In China, white sports of the Mallard had produced the Pekin, a more erect bird that has been used for the table for centuries. It was introduced to the USA in 1873 and initially became known there as the Long Island duck, a reference to the area in which it was raised commercially. The Pekin was introduced to Britain from 1874, with stock coming from both America and China. The American Pekin has not changed radically from the original importees, having a sturdy body carried at an angle of around 40 degrees. In Britain, it has been bred to be far more upright.

(Continued on Page 38)

Domestic Duck Breeds

(Illustrations by John Tarren)

Blue Swedish duck, a heavy breed with beautiful dark blue, laced plumage. It is difficult to breed well-marked birds of the right colour. Some of the young will be black or silver.

Abacot Ranger duck, a light breed with good egg production.

Buff Orpington duck, a light breed that was originally bred as a dual-purpose bird in Kent, using Indian Runner, Rouen and Aylesbury.

Silver Appleyard duck, a heavy breed that has a good record as a dual-purpose utility bird. There is also a miniature version.

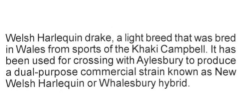

Welsh Harlequin drake, a light breed that was bred in Wales from sports of the Khaki Campbell. It has been used for crossing with Aylesbury to produce a dual-purpose commercial strain known as New Welsh Harlequin or Whalesbury hybrid.

36

Saxony drake

Saxony duck

Bred in Germany, the Saxony is a heavy breed with attractive markings and smooth plumage. it has been used as a dual-purpose breed for eggs and table. It needs plenty of space.

Pekin duck, an Asian breed that has been used all over the world as a source of table ducklings. In Britain it has been bred to be more upright than the original type.

Aylesbury drake. This is the breed that originally provided most of Britain's table ducks. It has been much crossed with Pekins to produce commercial strains. It needs water in order to mate.

Hook Bill drake. This was bred in the Netherlands with a curved bill and white bib so that wildfowlers could distinguish it in flight from the wild Mallard.

(More on pages 40-41)

The Pekin's head is round with full cheeks, giving the face a chubby appearance. The plumage is cream or deep cream, but the American standards specify white or creamy white only. The German Pekin has a more yellowish tinge.

The bill, legs and webs are bright orange, while the eyes are dark greyish blue. Typical weights are 4.1kg (9lb) for the male and 3.6kg (8lb) for the females. The eggs are yellowish white and more rounded than are the eggs of most breeds. This can lead to problems when it comes to artificial incubation. Average production is 150 eggs but commercial Pekins will lay far more.

Rouen

Rouen drake and duck
(Edward Brown, 1903)

(See page 40). This was the traditional table breed in France, and is named after the area in which it was bred. It has also been called the Rhone duck, the Rohan and the Roan. It was introduced to Britain in the early nineteenth century and was soon developed for size, usually by incorporating Aylesbury.

The Rouen resembles a large Mallard in its plumage, and is a colourful, attractive breed. The bill is greenish yellow with a black bean in the male, while that of the female is orange and black. The eyes are brown, while legs and webs are orange.

In its original or production form, the Rouen was smaller and more mobile than the massive standard-bred type that is required of today's exhibition birds. Its present size has undoubtedly affected its fertility so water mating is usually the only practical form of reproduction. It tends to start laying quite late, from March to early summer. Typical weights are 4.6 to 5.5kg (10-12lb) for the male and 4.1 to 5kg (9-11lb) for the females. Production is around 40 greenish or bluish eggs, but utility strains will lay up to around 120 a year.

The carriage, like that of the exhibition Aylesbury, is required to be horizontal, with the keel parallel to the ground. The British Waterfowl Standards state that the keel should actually *'touch the ground'*, while the American Standards require *'nearly touching the ground'*. My personal preference is for the older production type of Rouen that is able to walk about without dragging its keel along the ground, although it might not win any prizes at the show!

Rouen Clair

The Rouen Clair or Duclair also came from France and resembles the Mallard in its colouring, although it is lighter in hue. It is also more upright in stance and lighter in weight. Average weights are 3.4 to 4.1kg (7.5-9lb) for the male and 3 to 3.4kg (6.5-7.5lb) for the females. The eggs are white to greenish blue and average production is around 180 a year.

It is said to resemble the original Rouen before that was bred for a horizontal carriage in Britain. In this respect, it is interesting to note that in Belgium the Rouen is referred to as the Rouen Anglais, while the Rouen Clair is called the Rouen Francais.

38

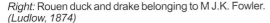

Above: Pekins on the left and Indian Runners on the right.
(Ludlow 1874)

Right: Rouen duck and drake belonging to M J.K. Fowler.
(Ludlow, 1874)

Cayuga

(Harrison Weir, 1898)

(See page 40). Before the Pekin was introduced to the USA, the Cayuga was the main table breed. It is named after Lake Cayuga in New York State where large black ducks were first recorded in 1850. It has glossy black plumage with a dark green sheen. The colour was probably improved by crossing with the smaller Black East Indian. In both sexes the bill, legs and webs are black, while the eyes are dark brown. Egg production is about 100 eggs a year. The shell colour can vary from white to dark green, while typical weights are 3.6kg (8lb) for the male and 3.2kg (7lb) for the female. In the USA, the Cayuga is classified as a medium weight breed.

Blue Swedish

Blue Swedish drake and duck
(P. Graham, 19th century)

(See page 36). The Blue Swedish is a beautiful bird, so-named from its rich blue plumage which is apparent in both sexes, although the male has a slight greenish lustre that is absent in the female. The feathers are well laced in darker blue and both sexes have a white bib. The outer primary feathers are also white. Average weights are 3.6kg (8lb) for the male and 3.2kg (7lb) for the female. The legs and webs are bluish-brown in the duck and orange-black in the drake. Ideally, the bill should be slate blue in both sexes, although it may be greenish in the male. The eyes are brown and egg production is about 100 blue or green-tinted eggs. It is difficult to breed good examples with the appropriate blue colour. Black and Lavender examples also appear, although these are not shown. In the USA, the Blue Swedish is known as the Swedish and is classified as a medium weight bird.

(Continued on Page 42)

Domestic Duck Breeds

Magpie, a light breed from Wales that was regarded as a dual-purpose bird. Good specimens have an all-white face, neck and underbody.

Cayuga drake, a heavy breed from the USA. *(John Tarren)*

Rouen duck, once the traditional table bird of France, but now mainly a show bird. *(John Tarren)*

Crested duck with a good, even crest. There is also a Miniature version. *(John Tarren)*

Black East Indian drake, an American bantam breed. *(John Tarren)*

Khaki Campbell drake. This breed is the best for egg production. *(John Tarren)*

Some of the author's White Call ducks. Their bills are too long to meet today's standards

Pied call ducks. Note the shorter bill. *(John Tarren).*

Black and White Muscovy. Here the markings are not regularly defined as the standards require.

White Indian Runners, traditionally the best layers before the Khaki Campbell was developed.

Chocolate Muscovy. *(John Tarren)*

Right: Muscovy ducks are excellent broodies. This one has hatched her brood in a rabbit hutch.

41

Pommern

Originating in Pomerania, the Pommern is slightly smaller than the Blue Swedish, and does not have the white primary or flight feathers that are found in the latter. It was the traditional farm duck in its area of origin, with a good reputation for quick growth. It has been bred pure in Switzerland since the 1920s. Weights are around 3kg (6.5lb) for the drake and 2.5kg (5.5lb) for the females. Egg production is around 150 a year and the shells are bluish-green.

There are two recognised colour strains in Germany. The Blue which is an even slate-blue colour, and the Black which is slate-black with a greenish hue. Both have white bibs. They are comparatively rare in Britain.

Shetland

The Shetland is also a version of the Blue Swedish, but the plumage is black rather than slate blue, and the laced markings are not as apparent, although there is a white bib. It is obvious that all the blue ducks - Blue Swedish, Pommern and Shetland - have a common ancestry, from the north sea coastal areas of Germany, Holland and Sweden.

Silver Appleyard

(See page 36). Originating in Britain, the Silver Appleyard was bred by Reginald Appleyard in the 1940s. His aim was to produce a big, dual-purpose, utility bird, beautifully marked and laying large white eggs. Unfortunately, the standard for the breed was lost and subsequent birds showed a considerable movement away from the originals. Fortunately, however, the waterfowl breeder Tom Bartlett was able to obtain a painting of the original Silver Appleyards from Mr Appleyard's daughter, and set to work to breed stock that resembled them.

Silver Appleyards are good dual-purpose ducks for table and eggs, as well as being most attractive in appearance. The drake has a dark green head and silvery white throat with a white ring around the neck. Its body plumage colouring includes claret, white, silver grey, dark green, and a distinctive blue speculum. The female is creamy white with greyish brown on the flanks and back. She also has the blue speculum and a distinctive eye stripe. Both sexes have yellow bills, brown eyes and orange legs and webs. Depending on the strain, egg production is 150-200 whitish eggs.

Saxony

(See page 37). This attractive breed, with its unusual colouring and soft, close plumage, was first developed in the Saxony region of Germany in the 1930s but was subsequently re-made in the 1950s, using Rouen, German Pekin and Blue Pommern. It was developed as a dual-purpose, utility breed producing good weights for the table as well as around 150 eggs a year. Weights are 3.6kg (8lb) for the male and 3.2kg (7lb) for the female.

The Muscovy has retained its ability to fly, hence its appearance in the wild on many ponds.

The drake's head and neck are a soft grey-blue (sometimes referred to as pigeon blue) with a white ring that encircles the neck. Its lower neck and breast are rusty red, with silver lacing, while its lower parts are oatmeal coloured.The rump, tail feathers and flight feathers are greyish blue, with a darker speculum. (The latter is the name given to the electric-blue secondary feathers of the Mallard).

The duck, in my view, is even more attractive, with a soft apricot head, neck and breast. There is no neck ring, although the throat is white, but there are distinctive eye stripes. The wing tips and speculum are grey-blue. Both sexes have dark brown eyes, a yellow bill and orange legs and webs.

Muscovy (See page 41). The Muscovy, as referred to earlier, is from an entirely different genetic line to other domestic ducks. It is a perching duck, related to

Muscovy drake and duck. *(Harrison Weir)*

the South American tree duck, *Cairina moschata*. With domestication, it has been developed for increased weight, as well as a range of colouring from the original all-black duck. Other names by which it has been called in the past include, Musk duck, Brazilian, Barbary and Peruvian. Unlike the males of domestic breeds, the male Muscovy does not have curled tail feathers. There is a considerable difference in the size of the sexes, with males averaging 4.6 to 6.4kg (10-14lb), while females are 2.3-3.2kg (5-7lb), although the carriage in both sexes is horizontal.

(Continued on Page 46)

43

Commercial Duck Breeds

Cherry Valley SM3 table duck, developed in Britain.

Grimaud Frères range of table ducks in France.
From left to right: Hytop Mule, Canedin and Grimaud Option.

Golden 300 hybrid layers developed at Metzer Farms in California.

Table ducks being reared in Asia. The water flows through the house with its individual pens and ensures that they do not suffer from heat stress.
(International Hatchery Practice)

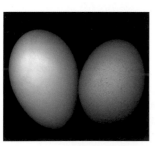

Comparison of a duck egg and a hen's egg.
The one on the left is from a Khaki Campbell duck while the one on the right is a Speckledy hen's egg.

Gourmaud Selection ST14 Barbarie, developed for the free-range Label Rouge sector in France.

One of the author's New Welsh Harlequins or Whalesbury hybrids bred from Welsh Harlequin and Aylesbury. It proved to be an excellent dual-purpose strain for table and eggs.

Ducklings of the Kortlang strain of Khaki Campbell egg layer. This is the prime layer in Britain, capable of producing well over 300 eggs in a season. It is popular with smallholders for its ability to lay in winter when hen eggs may be in short supply.

The body is broad and powerful, with short, strong legs and webs that have pronounced claws, as befits a climbing duck. The head is large with a crest that is raised when the bird is alarmed. The face has red caruncles or fleshy protuberances that project slightly over the base of the bill. Although both sexes have crests and caruncle, they are more pronounced in the male.

A notable feature of the Muscovy is the absence of a 'quack'. It hisses or puffs, a characteristic that those with close neighbours might welcome. One of our drakes was called Jeremiah (from the old rhyme *Jeremiah, Obadiah, Huff Puff Puff*).

Another feature is that it has retained the ability to fly, although this is more marked when the birds are young. Once they have settled down in a particular place, they are less likely to fly away.

The Muscovy is an excellent table bird and lays large, white eggs with deep yellow yolks. It is also a good broody that can always be relied upon to hatch and rear a clutch of eggs. The male can occasionally be aggressive and may mate with other breeds, although the progeny are invariably sterile and are called Mules. There are several colour varieties, including Black, Black and White, White-winged Black, Blue, Blue and White, White-winged Blue, Chocolate, Chocolate and White, White-winged Chocolate, and White. In the USA, the following varieties are recognised: White, Coloured, Blue, and Chocolate.

Light breeds

In the nineteenth century, with the importation of Indian Runners into Britain and elsewhere, a greater emphasis was placed on the egg producing capacity of ducks than had hitherto been the case. It was also perceived that as ducks are hardier than chickens, they are able to withstand colder temperatures and will lay in winter if provided with the right conditions. They could provide eggs when chickens might have stopped laying, so effectively filling in the gap.

Indian Runner   (See page 41). Indian Runners were first introduced to Britain by a ship's captain who brought some white, fawn, and fawn and white ducks back from Malaya. They were notable for their upright 'penguin' type stance and also for their egg laying abilities. An extremely lively bird, the Runner certainly lives up to its name. A flock of them will also move at an extremely fast pace, all moving together, first this way and then that, in unison. It is no coincidence that they are sometimes used to demonstrate the skills of sheepdogs in agricultural shows, rather than the more usual sheep.

Prize Indian Runners.
(Harrison Weir, 19thC).

A prolific egg layer, the Indian Runner has been used in the production of many of our light breeds, including the Khaki Campbell, Orpington, Welsh Harlequin and Magpie. Since the first introductions, the breed has been bred for an even more perpendicular stance, with a recommended length from bill to toe tip of 65-80cm for the drake and 60-70cm for the duck. Harrison Weir's drawing, on page 46, of some prize Indian Runners in the 19th century shows a more horizontal carriage. Weights are 1.6 to 2.3kg (3.5-5lb) for the male and 1.4 to 2.1kg (3-4.5lb) for the female. The eggs are mainly white, although there may be some with a greenish hue. Around 200 eggs a year are laid.

The following colour varieties are recognised in Britain: White, Black, Chocolate, Cumberland Blue, Fawn, Fawn and White, American Fawn and White, Trout, and Mallard. In the USA, the following are recognised: White, Fawn and White, Black, Pencilled, Buff, Chocolate, Cumberland Blue, and Gray.

Campbell

(See page 40). In 1901, a Mrs Campbell from Uley in Gloucestershire bred the Khaki Campbell, using a Rouen drake on Fawn and White Runner ducks, with some additions from the wild Mallard to give increased hardiness. Very similar ducks had also been bred in Holland. It is certainly the case that the Tonsul duck from Holland was used by *Kortlang*, the breeder of commercial layers, to improve productivity.

The olive-brown bird proved to be a first rate layer, outperforming the Runner which had been the best layer until then. Commercial strains of Khaki Campbell still hold the record for egg production which can be as high as 350 eggs per annum, although around 200 is more likely for non-commercial strains. Eggs are large and white with a slight greenish hue, while average weights are 2.3-2.5kg (5-5.5lb) for the male and 2.1 to 2.3kg (4.5-5lb) for the female. They are also early maturing, coming into lay at around 26 weeks, but earlier for commercial strains. They have healthy appetites and need good feeding to produce well.

The White Campbell was originally a sport or random mutation of the Khaki Campbell. A Captain Pardoe had some in 1924, while a Mr Peasgood also developed them in the 1950s, calling them White Warwickshires after his home county. It was subsequently used in the development of the Abacot Ranger. In Britain, the Dark Campbell was bred by Mr H. Humphreys of Devon, so that sex linkage as a means of determining sex at hatching was possible. (The males are darker). It was also developed in Germany where it is called the German Campbell.

Crested

(See page 40). The origin of the Crested duck is unknown, although it was probably a fairly common mutation in farmyard flocks all over Europe. It has been depicted in 17th century Dutch paintings. The gene for a crest is associated with skeletal deformities, so breeding good examples of Crested ducks can be difficult.

The crests may also range from a full, fluffy ball to a small bump with a few feathers. In Britain, the recognised varieties are White, and Coloured (ie, any other colour). In the USA, the Crested is classified as a medium weight breed, and two varieties are recognised: the White and the Black. Average weights are 3.2kg (7lb) for the male and 2.7kg (6lb) for the female. Eggs are white, sometimes tinted with blue or green.

Crested duck.
(Harrison Weir, 1902)

47

Ornamental Duck Breeds

Tufted duck, a diving breed that feeds on organisms in the mud at the bottom.

Carolina drake, a wood duck and native of North America but a popular sight in many collections.

Fulvous Whistling duck), a handsome breed that is more hardy than others of its kind.

A concrete pond made for a range of ornamental ducks.

Ornamental ducks need nesting sites that are appropriate to the specific breed.

Ornamental duck shelters and nesting boxes suitable for wood ducks such as Mandarins and Carolinas. *(Forsham Cottage Arks)*

European Shelduck, a large grazing duck that can be aggressive to smaller breeds. They are more suitable for large areas.

The beautifully marked Mandarin drake, a wood duck native to China but now living wild in parts of Britain. It nests in holes in trees or other raised sites.

European Wigeon, a dabbler that feeds on pond plants as well as grasses and marginal plants.

Mallards, such as this drake and duck soon populate a large pond or lake, whether you like it or not.

Broody hens are effective at hatching and brooding ducklings, both utility and ornamental.

Waterfowl that hatch their own eggs will ensure that the young are preened with oil before they go onto the water.

Abacot Ranger (See page 36).

Originally called the Hooded Ranger from its head and neck plumage which resembled a hood, this breed was bred by Oscar Gray of Colchester during and after World War 1. Bred from a light-coloured sport of Khaki Campbell and White Indian Runner, it was seen as a step towards the goal of producing a dual-purpose duck. After the 1920s, the breed seems to have disappeared, although similarly marked strains were developed in Wales as the Welsh Harlequin by Leslie Bonnet. (See later). Meanwhile, the breed apparently continued in Germany as the Streicher duck. As this had the features of the original, the present standards for the Abacot Ranger are a translation from the German.

Average weights are 2.5-2.7kg (5.5-6lb) for the male and 2.3-2.5kg (5-5.5lb) for the female. The eggs are large and white. Good examples can lay over 250 eggs.

Orpington (See page 36)

The Orpington was bred in Kent by William Cook, who also bred the Orpington chicken. The breeding included Indian Runner, Rouen and Aylesbury. Mr Cook's aim was to produce a dual-purpose breed for eggs and the table, but it is now classified as a light breed. It is a most attractive bird with buff coloured plumage. The male is a richer buff than the female and has a dark brown head and neck. In the USA, the breed is recognised as the Buff and is classified as a medium weight bird.

Average weights are 2.2-3.4kg (5-7.5lb) for the males and 2.2 to 3.2 (5-7lb) for the female. Egg production is around 150 white eggs a year, although good specimens can produce more. There is also a Blue Orpington, but as the numbers are low, it is not yet recognised.

Magpie (See page 40)

Bred in Wales, the Magpie was originally a dual-purpose breed on the hill farms, but is now classified as a light breed. Its plumage is white, with a black cap and black back from shoulders to tail. The legs and bill are yellow. There are also Blue and White, and Dun and White varieties. Average weights are 2.5-3.2kg (5.5-7lb) for the drake and 2-2.7kg (4.5-6lb) for the duck. Egg production is around 150 eggs, but selective breeding would improve this. It is difficult to breed birds with good clear markings, but it is an attractive breed that is well worth the effort. A similar variety, the Altrhein Magpie has been developed in Germany.

Welsh Harlequin (See page 36)

Bred by Mr Leslie Bonnet in the mid-1940s, the Welsh Harlequin has had a somewhat chequered career. The original birds were developed from sports of the Khaki Campbell, but were subsequently crossed with Aylesbury for greater weight, to produce the Whalesbury hybrid. After losing most of his flock to foxes, Mr Bonnet amalgamated the remaining Welsh Harlequins with Whalesbury hybrids, calling them New Welsh Harlequins. I bought some of these from the Harlequin Duck Farm in North

Wales, in the 1970s, when they were sold as Welsh Harlequins. They were beautiful honey-coloured birds, laid well and made excellent table birds. Unfortunately, our breeding flock was stolen one night, probably by an unscrupulous breeder, after I had described them in a magazine article. In the 1980s, the Welsh Harlequin Duck Club was formed, following the discovery that Mr Eddie Grayson had purchased a small number of Leslie Bonnet's original Welsh Harlequins in the 1960s. A new standard was then drawn

Some of the author's New Welsh Harlequins before they were stolen.

up for the breed. Average weights now are 2.3-2.5kg (5-5.5lb) for the male and 2-2.3kg 4.5-5lb) for the female. Eggs are white with a potential production of around 250 a year.

Bali

Originating in the East Indies, this light breed takes its name from the island of Bali. It was introduced to Britain in the 1920s but was recently re-created from crosses of Crested and Indian Runner. In appearance, it is like an Indian Runner with a crest, and may be all-white or any colour. It is regarded primarily as a show bird, although it is capable of producing around 180 eggs a year.

Hook Bill   A native of Asia, the White-Bibbed Hook Bill was developed in the Netherlands, where it appears in old paintings, and seems to have been widespread throughout northern and eastern Europe. The characteristic white bib and curved

Bow Bill.
(*Mrs Beeton*, 1859)

bill were developed so that, in flight, it could be distinguished from the wild Mallard. A bow-billed breed was well known to Mrs Beeton as the illustration from her cookery book shows. (See left). It has also been called the Crook Bill. It was re-introduced to Britain in the 1980s and 1990s and is now called the Hook Bill. (There is no crest). Recognised varieties include the White, Dark Mallard and White-Bibbed Dark Mallard. Average weights are 2.3-2.5kg (5-5.5lb) for the male and 1.8-2.3kg (3.25-5lb) for the female.

Mallard

Reference has already been made to the fact that all breeds of domestic ducks, with the exception of the Muscovy, are descended from the wild Mallard. It is also our most common wild duck and will often visit or take up residence on ponds and lakes, whether we like it or not. It will breed with other species of the *Anas* group, and precautions must be taken to exclude other breeds from its attentions if crossings are to be avoided. There are many incidences of wild ducks which are the result of such liasons. The photograph on page 11 shows some examples. It would be wrong however, to think of the Mallard as a mere nuisance. It is attractive in its own right and, as with any species, represents a valuable genetic source. It has also been used for commercial purposes in the production of the Gressingham duck. (See Commercial breeds).

There are two species of the wild Mallard: the Northerm Mallard, *Anas platyrhynchos platyrhynchos*, and the Greenland Mallard, *Anas platyrhynchos conboschas*. In the USA, there is a standard for the Mallard. It has been developed from the wild Mallard of North America and is classified as a bantam. There are two varieties; the Gray and the Snowy. In Britain, the Mallard is not recognised as a domestic breed, but as a native wildfowl.

Bantam, Miniature and Call ducks

There are some breeds that are naturally small, while some have been bred as miniature versions of larger ducks. They are normally kept as show breeds, although an increasing number of people are now keeping them as pets in their gardens. It is important to remember that the small breeds are capable of flight.

Call ducks

Call ducks.
(Mrs Beeton, 1859)

(See page 41). In the British Standards, Call ducks have their own classification of *Calls*, while in the USA, they are classified as *Bantams*. They are the smallest of the domestic duck breeds. Although originating in Asia and first imported into the Netherlands, they were standardized in Britain. The old name of Decoy ducks or Coys refers to the fact that they were widely used as lures to attract wildfowl onto lakes where they could be trapped. They are small, compact birds, that have frequently been described as typical 'rubber ducks'. Alert and quick, they are popular with many, although close neighbours may not always appreciate their excitable quacking. The following varieties are recognised in Britain: White, Bibbed, Apricot, Pied, Blue Fawn, Silver, Dark Silver, Magpie, and Mallard (also called Brown or Grey). In the USA, the following are recognised: Gray, White, Blue, and Snowy. Average weights are 0.6-0.7kg (1.25-1.5lb) for the drake and 0.5-0.6kg (1-1.25lb) for the duck. Egg numbers are not great. They are best kept in pairs or trios and can become very tame.

Black East Indian   (See page 40). This American bantam has had several names in the past, including Black Brazilian and Labrador. Mrs Beeton referred to it as the Buenos Aires. It is thought to have originated as a black sport of the Mallard

Buenos Aires ducks.
(Mrs Beeton, 1859)

and is a neat little duck with glossy black plumage with a greenish sheen. Average weights are 0.9kg (2lb) for the drake and 0.7-0.8kg (1.5-1.75lb) for the duck. The breed is thought to have been used in order to improve the colour of the Cayuga. It is not a prolific layer and can be difficult to breed. There is a Blue version that is not recognised. In the USA, the Black East Indian is called East India.

52

Silver Appleyard Miniature
These miniature versions of the Silver Appleyard were bred in Britain by Tom Bartlett in the 1980s. Weights are 1.4kg (3lb) for the male and 1.1kg (2.5lb) for the duck.

Silver Bantam
This was bred in Britain by Reginald Appleyard in the 1940s. It was produced from a White Call drake crossed with a small Khaki Campbell duck, and was originally called the Silver Appleyard Bantam. Average weights are 0.9kg (2lb) for the drake and 0.8kg (1.75lb) for the duck.

Crested Miniature
Bred in Britain in the 1980s-1990s, the Crested Miniature is a replica of its larger counterpart, except of course for size. Average weights are 1.1kg (2.5lb) for the male and 0.9kg (2lb) for the female.

Commercial breeds

For commercial purposes, hybrid strains tend to be used because their production is superior to most pure-bred stock. Where pure-bred stock and hybrid strains are kept, it is obviously important to prevent inter-breeding, unless it is for a specific reason.

Most hybrid table ducks are based on the Pekin, Aylesbury and Muscovy, while egg producers are based on the Khaki Campbell and White Indian Runner. The strains were (and often are) given names by their breeders. For example, the Pennine duck was a hybrid based on the Pekin, with some Aylesbury input, that was produced in the north of England by Will Bradley and Thornbers. The Whalesbury hybrid, referred to earlier, was a cross between Welsh Harlequin and Aylesbury. The Gressingham duck, also referred to earlier, was the name given to a strain of wild Mallard raised for the table so that the meat had a more 'gamey' flavour. Other examples are shown below.

Kortlang (See page 45)
Famous for its commercial laying strains of Khaki Campbell, Kortlangs started in the Netherlands but has been in Britain since before World War 2. The company has developed high-laying Kortlang strains capable of producing up to 350 eggs a season.

Cherry Valley (See page 44)
Cherry Valley produces both laying ducks and table birds, although they are best known for the latter. Their Cherry Valley 2000 egg layer is a hybrid strain based on the White Runner, while their table bird Cherry Valley SM3 is a fast-growing strain. They supply breeding stock as well as ducks for rearing.

Gourmaud Sélection (See page 45)
Based in France, this company has a range that they call Barbarie ducks, based on hybrid crossings of the Muscovy. Of particular interest is their Gourmaud Sélection ST14 Barbarie, a compact, grey-feathered duck that was developed for the *Label Rouge* free-range sector. They also have white and grey Mule (sterile) ducks that are Pekins crossed with one of their Barbarie strains for table duck production.

Grimaud Frères (See page 44)

Also in France, Grimaud, have used their Pekin and Muscovy lines to develop a range of table ducks to suit particular requirements, including free-range. Their Canedin Muscovy lines are available in different colours for raising or crossing. Grimaud Option is a Pekin-based strain producing around 230 eggs, while Hytop Mule is a table bird from crossing Option Pekin with a Canedin Muscovy line.

Nordam Breeders

This is a Danish company that produces the Broholm Berlill table duck based on the Legarth strain of commercial Pekin.

Metzer (See page 44)

The American company Metzer sells pure breeds as well as hybrids. It has also developed its own prolific layer called the Golden 300 hybrid

Ornamental breeds

Ornamental breeds are more difficult to keep because of their differing environmental needs, so it is a good idea to visit collections, talk to breeders and consider becoming a member of the British Waterfowl Association which offers a great deal of useful advice and information.

An important aspect to bear in mind is that native species do not need to be kept confined, so if they escape, you will not be liable to prosecution. This is not to say that they should not receive the same anti-fox protection as domestic breeds if they are kept in a collection. The 1981 *Countryside and Wildlife Act* specifies that it is an offence to release non-indigenous breeds into the wild. There are sound reasons for this: they may be aggressive to native ducks to the extent that a decline in numbers of native species may result. The escape into the wild of the North American Ruddy Ruck, *Oxyra jamaicensis*, is an example of this.

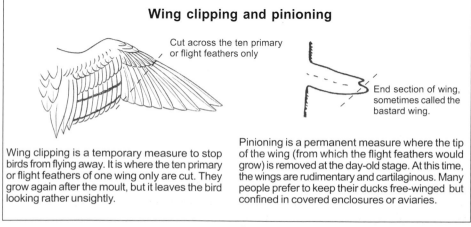

Wing clipping and pinioning

Cut across the ten primary or flight feathers only

End section of wing, sometimes called the bastard wing.

Wing clipping is a temporary measure to stop birds from flying away. It is where the ten primary or flight feathers of one wing only are cut. They grow again after the moult, but it leaves the bird looking rather unsightly.

Pinioning is a permanent measure where the tip of the wing (from which the flight feathers would grow) is removed at the day-old stage. At this time, the wings are rudimentary and cartilaginous. Many people prefer to keep their ducks free-winged but confined in covered enclosures or aviaries.

Examples of nest boxes for ornamentals
(See also page 48)

A raised nest box with ramp suitable for climbing ornamentals.

Ground nest with 'tunnel' access in an aviary.

A wooden nest box with 'tunnel' access. *Warners.*

'Decorative house' nest box on a concrete island with ramps. (Part of a children's area in a waterfowl collection).

There are three ways of ensuring that escape into the wild does not take place - by wing clipping, pinioning or keeping them in an aviary. The first is not really appropriate for it would need to be done every year. Many people are understandably reluctant to pinion birds unless it is absolutely necessary, because it does mean that their ability to fly is removed permanently. Many breeds will adapt well to aviary conditions, as long as the aviary is big enough, has a shelter and nesting area within it, and has a pond with the requisite depth of water. It is customary for some small breeds, such as the Hottentot Teal and the Ringed Teal to be kept free-winged (unpinioned) in an aviary. The Hottentot is the smallest breed of duck.

Reference has already been made to the differing water depth needed, depending on whether the ducks are dabblers or divers. Perching ducks will obviously need tree cover and perching places. Large aviaries should have room for appropriate trees or shrubs for this purpose. Some suitable varieties are listed in the table on page 57.

It is important to remember that imported breeds may not be winter hardy, so must be provided with adequate winter shelter in the aviary or enclosure. Whistling ducks, for example, are not particularly hardy, although the Fulvous Whistling duck is hardier than other members of the group. A house or simple shelter within the aviary can be positioned so that it is facing away from the prevailing wind. The webbed feet of non-hardy ornamentals are particularly prone to frost damage, so it is vital to avoid letting them go onto ponds that are likely to freeze.

Some breeds require specific conditions that may be beyond the capabilities of the general or beginner duck keeper. These include the Eider, the Goldeneyes and the Scoters which require high protein diets to compensate for the possible lack of fish and crustaceans in the diet. The so-called 'sea ducks' that are used to salt water may also suffer from sinus and other infections in normal ponds and lakes. In some collections, for example, Eiders are often given their food in a trough containing salt water, on the bank. Only experienced duck keepers are advised to try this, for it is easy to overdo the salinity. It should be remembered that excess salt is toxic to most ducks.

Nesting requirements

Provision must be made for nesting requirements, and these vary depending on the type of ducks. Ground nesting birds, such as the Tufted duck and the European Pochard, need fairly dense vegetation in the form of reeds, tall grasses or bushes, although they will accept wooden nest boxes. Some prefer slightly underground nests with a 'tunnel' or pipe access such as the example shown on the previous page. This type of nest also prevents predatory corvids, such as crows and magpies, stealing the eggs. If a nest seems to be particularly vulnerable in this respect, it is a good idea to 'build' a shelter of branches, or other supporting structure over which a canopy can be placed.

Carolinas on the left and Mandarins on the right.
(Ludlow, 1874)

In the wild, perchers such as the Mandarin and Carolina, nest in holes in trees. They therefore need to be provided with raised nest boxes. Even a section of old barrel wedged in a tree may prove acceptable, or there are purpose-made ones available from suppliers.

The table on pages 58-59 gives details of the type of nest required by different ornamental ducks, while the table opposite shows some of the plants that can be used for both sheltering and nesting purposes.

56

Plants for the Pond, Aviary and Enclosure

Plant	Purpose
Bamboo, *Phyllostachys sp.*	Ornamental; shelter; nesting
Bogbean, *Menyanthes trifoliata*	Ornamental marginal
Box, *Buxus sp.*	Shelter
Rushes, *Scirpus sp.*	Ornamental; shelter; nesting
Canadian Pondweed, *Elodea canadensis*	Oxygenating plant for ponds
Chinese Juniper, *Juniperus chinensis pfitzneriana*	Ornamental; shelter; perching; nesting
Reeds, *Phragmites sp.*	Shelter; nesting; ornamental
Dogwood, *Cornus sp.*	Shelter; ornamental
Duckweed, *Lemna minor*	Food plant in ponds
Dwarf Pine, *Pinus mugo pumilio*	Shelter; perching; nesting; ornamental
Juncus Reeds, *Juncus sp.*	Shelter; nesting; ornamental
Marsh Marigold, *Caltha palustris*	Ornamental marginal plant
Pampas Grass, *Cotaderia sp.*	Shelter; nesting; ornamental
Sedges, *Carex sp.*	Nesting; shelter; ornamental
Watercress, *Nasturtium officinale*	Food marginal plant
Willowherb, *Epilobium hirsutum*	Shelter; nesting; ornamental.
Yellow Flag Iris, *Iris pseudacorus*	Shelter; nesting, ornamental.

Breeds for the beginner

The following dabbling breeds do not pose any great difficulty for the beginner: Common Shoveler, Gadwall, Northern Pintail, most Teal and European Wigeon, although it should be remembered that the latter is also a grazer and needs access to short grasses.

Divers which will require deeper water, but are otherwise easy to keep include the Tufted duck and European Pochard, although the latter is happiest in larger expanses of water, not just that which is deeper.

Perching ducks that are relatively easy to keep are Mandarin and Carolina. These two breeds are amongst the most popular because of their colourful plumage and equable temperaments. The Carolina, however, is a non-indigenous breed and legally needs to be kept confined.

To detail *all* the ornamental duck breeds is beyond the scope of this book, but the table on pages 58-59 gives basic information about the various types and their needs, as well as nesting and incubation details. Those marked with an * are the non-indigenous breeds that are required to be confined. The BWA has leg rings that can be used for the identification of specific birds.

Ornamental breeds of ducks

Species	Nesting period and requirements	Comments
* Australian Wood duck (Maned goose) *Chenonetta jubata*	March-May. 28 days. Ground nest box or partly underground with pipe or tunnel entrance.	Percher. Needs branches. Fairly easy to breed but not winter hardy
* Baikal Teal, *Anas formosa.* (Speckled or Formosa teal)	April-May. 24 days. Natural cover. Ground nest.	Colourful plumage. Easy to keep but can be difficult to breed.
* Blue Winged Teal *Anas discors*	April-May. 23 days. Natural cover. Ground nest.	Dabbler. Easy to breed. Co-exists readily with other breeds.
* Cape Teal, *Anas capensis*	April-May. 25 days. Natural cover. Ground nest.	Easy to breed. Suitable for beginner. Colourful all year.
* Carolina, *Aix sponsa* (North American Wood duck)	March-June. 30 days. Raised or ground box.	Percher. Needs branches. Easy to breed. Suitable for beginner.
* Chestnut Breasted Teal *Anas castanea*	April-May. 28 days. Natural cover. Ground or raised nest box.	Dabbler. Easy to breed.
* Chilean Teal, *Anas flavirostris*	April-May. 24 days. Natural cover. Ground or raised box.	Dabbler. Easy to breed. Gentle disposition.
* Chiloe Wigeon *Anas sibilatrix*	April-June. 26 days. Natural cover. Ground or raised box.	Dabbler/grazer. Easy to breed. Suitable for beginner.
* Cinnamon Teal, *Anas cyanoptera septentrionalium*	April-May. 23 days. Natural cover. Ground nest.	Easy to breed. Suitable for beginner.
Common (European) Shelduck *Tadorna tadorna*	April-May. 30 days. Undergound nest box with pipe entrance or ground box.	Easy to breed. Omnivorous. May be aggressive to smaller ducks. Will fly away if not confined or pinioned.
Common (European or Northern) Shoveler *Anas clypeata*	April-May. 25 days. Natural cover. Ground nest.	Dabbler. Fairly easy to breed. In captivity needs a high protein diet. Will fly away if not confined.
European Green Winged Teal (Common Teal) *Anas crecca*	April-May. 22 days. Natural cover. Ground nest box.	Dabbler. Can be difficult to breed. Will fly away if not confined.
* European Goldeneye *Bucephala clangula*	March-May. 30 days. Raised nest box.	Diver. Fairly easy to breed but needs a high protein diet and a large area of water. Not for beginner.
European Pochard *Aythya ferina*	April-May. 25 days. Natural cover. Ground or raised nest.	Diver. Fairly easy to breed. Needs large expanse of water.
European Wigeon *Anas penelope*	April-June. 24 days. Natural cover. Ground nest box.	Dabbler/grazer. Fairly easy to breed. Needs short grass for grazing.
* Falcated Teal, *Anas falcata*	April-June. 25 days. Natural cover. Ground nest box.	Dabbler. Fairly easy to breed.
* Fulvous Tree (Whistling) duck *Dendrocygna bicolor*	April-June. 30 days. Natural cover. Ground or raised box.	Percher. Vegetarian/grazer. Hardiest breed of whistling duck. Easy to breed but may bully smaller ducks. Not for beginner.
Gadwall, *Anas strepera*	April-May. 26 days. Natural cover. Ground nest.	Dabbler. Easy to breed.

Species	Nesting period and requirements	Comments
Garganey, *Anas querquedula* (Summer Teal)	April-May. 23 days. Natural cover. Ground box.	Dabbler. Can be difficult to breed. Needs winter protection.
* Hottentot Teal, *Anas punctata*	April-May. 25 days. Natural cover. Ground or raised box.	Easy to breed. The smallest breed. Best kept free-winged in an aviary.
* Lesser Bahama Pintail *Anas bahamensis*	April-May. 25 days. Natural cover. Ground box.	Easy to breed. Suitable for beginner.
Mallard, *Anas platyrhynchos*	Feb-July. 28 days. Natural cover. Ground or raised box.	Dabbler. Easy to breed. Will cross-breed with domestic breeds.
Mandarin, *Aix galericulata*	March-June. 29 days. Raised nest box.	Percher. Easy to breed. Suitable for beginner.
* Marbled Teal *Anas angustirostris*	April-June. 25 days. Raised nest box.	Difficult to breed.
Northern Pintail, *Anas acuta* (Common Pintail)	April-May. 24 days. Natural cover. Ground nest box.	Dabbler. Easy to breed. Suitable for beginner, but will fly away unless confined.
* Philippine duck, *Anas luzonica*	April-May. 28 days.	Dabbler. Easy to breed. Suitable for beginner.
* Red Crested Pochard *Netta rufina*	April-May. 28 days. Natural cover. Ground nest box.	Diver. Easy to breed. Vegetarian. Needs grass. Suitable for beginner.
* Ringed Teal *Anas leucophrys*	April-June. 26 days. Raised nest box.	Easy to breed. Best kept free-winged in an aviary.
* Spotbilled duck *Anas poecilorhyncha*	April-May. 27 days. Natural cover. Ground nest.	Dabbler. Relatively easy to breed.
* Silver Teal, *Anas versicolor*	April-May. 25 days. Natural cover. Ground nest.	Dabbler. Fairly easy to breed.
Tufted duck, *Anas fuligula*	April-June. 24 days. Natural cover. Ground nest.	Diver. Easy to breed. Suitable for beginner.

The breeds indicated are the some of the ones most commonly kept in waterfowl collections, but there are many others. It is a good idea to go and view collections that are open to the public.

The ones marked with * are those that are required to be kept confined - by pinioning or enclosing in an aviary - otherwise the owners are liable to prosecution if they escape.

Beginners are recommended to start with native breeds only, where this legislation does not apply, although some sort of confinement such as an aviary or covered enclosure is necessary otherwise they will fly away. Keeping breeds in pairs or trios helps to prevent them from leaving a site.

Further information is available from the British Waterfowl Association.

Buying stock

Grufydd Elis, druan dro,
Aeth i'r ffair i werthu llo;
Dwad adref ar gefn hwyaden.
(Traditional Welsh rhyme)

Grufydd Elis, poor old soul,
Went to the fair to sell a calf,
But came back home on the back of a duck.

With all the relevant information about breeds, and with the housing and pond prepared, it is now time to buy some ducks. If the choice is for one of the domestic breeds, with the emphasis on pure-bred stock, it is a good idea to have a copy of the breed standards for the breed concerned, so that potential buys can be compared with the ideal. Individual breed clubs will have these details, while all the breeds are illustrated and described in the *British Waterfowl Standards*, published by the British Waterfowl Association. Another organisation which caters for domestic breeds and produces a list of breeders is the Domestic Waterfowl Club of Great Britain. Details of both organisations are in the Reference section.

If commercial strains of domestic ducks are the choice, because eggs or table qualities are the priority, it is worth asking the breeder for production records.

If the choice is to be ornamentals, the BWA is again a good source of information and advice. It produces an excellent newsletter and yearbook for its members.

As far as making contact with breeders is concerned, the monthly magazine *Country Smallholding* publishes a Breeders' Directory in every issue. It is also on their website at www.countrysmallholding.com, and there is an on-line bookshop. The BWA also has a Breeders' Directory which includes breeders of domestic and ornamental breeds. Their website has a useful on-line shop for books, videos and supplies such as leg rings for identification of specific birds.

Healthy birds

It goes without saying that birds should be healthy with an alert stance and good carriage. Illness is often reflected in a drooping posture and a dull rather glazed expression about the eyes. Conversely, a highly strung, nervous duck will tend to be hyperactive and panic easily.

The feathers should have a healthy sheen to them. Ragged plumage may be an indication of parasitic worm infestation, although it is worth remembering that a bird will often look a bit ragged when it is moulting. Some heavy breeds, such as the Muscovy, are prone to a slipped wing condition. This is the result of muscular weakness, where the wing droops down rather than being held along the side of the body. Sometimes it may even project outwards. (See the photograph on page 90). No breeding should take place from such birds, for there is some evidence that it is a hereditary condition. It can also be caused by too much protein when the duck is growing.

What to look for in a healthy duck

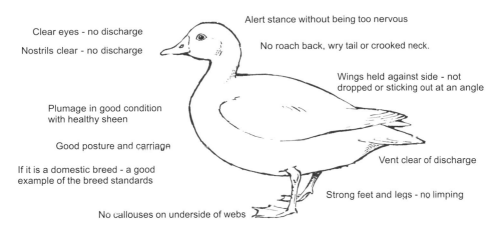

Clear eyes - no discharge

Nostrils clear - no discharge

Alert stance without being too nervous

No roach back, wry tail or crooked neck.

Wings held against side - not dropped or sticking out at an angle

Plumage in good condition with healthy sheen

Good posture and carriage

If it is a domestic breed - a good example of the breed standards

Vent clear of discharge

Strong feet and legs - no limping

No callouses on underside of webs

The legs and feet should be strong, with no evidence of limping or callouses on the webs. Check the bill and vent for any evidence of discharge which may indicate disease. Watch out for the presence of a roach back which indicates a spine curvature. The tail should be straight rather than displaced to the side, and the neck should also be nice and straight.

Any newly bought ducks should be placed in quarantine for 10 days before they are introduced to other ducks. This period allows any incubating diseases to manifest in conditions where they will not be passed on to other birds. Commercially, where ducks are being reared for the table, or as egg producers, it is best to avoid mixing old and new birds.

Age and availability

The age at which to buy will depend on the enterprise. Table ducks, for example will usually be purchased as newly hatched ducklings, unless breeding stock has been bought for raising your own. Utility layers are available as newly hatched ducklings, those from 6 weeks of age, or those that are approaching point-of-lay. Laying usually starts between 21-26 weeks old, but often earlier for commercial hybrids.

Pure-bred, domestic ducks are usually available as ducklings once they are hardy, or as older birds if they are required for breeding. Try and ensure that males and females come from different lines so that there is less chance of the young being born with congenital defects.

Occasionally it is possible to buy fertile eggs, but this is usually on a localized basis. It is worth bearing in mind that the younger the stock, the more care they will need in the vulnerable stage until they are hardy.

Finally, some ducks, particularly some ornamental breeds, may be in short supply, a situation that is often reflected in the price. There may also be a waiting list!

Feeding

They gobble it up, they swish their tails,
They stamp and quack with glee:
Beware the sight of the Pirate Ducks
When they're out on a raiding spree. (Honor Gasston, 1985)

All ducks, whether dabblers, divers or perchers, have the same need for nutrients in the form of proteins, carbohydrates, fats, minerals and vitamins; it is merely the proportions and the form in which they are found or presented that vary.

A balanced diet is essential, for too much of one type of food at the expense of other nutrients can soon lead to problems. The fact that people often throw bread to ducks on public park ponds does not mean that this is their sole diet. This is not to say that bread cannot be given, but it should be an occasional rather than a regular item. Dried bread should be broken into small pieces and soaked, for choking is not unheard of. It is also vital to ensure that any bread given is free of moulds. The ideal diet is a compound ration with all the necessary nutrients.

Compound feeds

Compound feeds normally consist of wheat and maize, with soya bean meal and soya oil added in order to provide the extra protein and energy requirements. Minerals and vitamins are also added to ensure against deficiencies. They are formulated in several forms, depending on the age of the birds and whether they are domestic or ornamental breeds. Many ornamentals, for example, need a higher protein level because they are used to feeding on insect larvae and crustaceans in the water. Some feeds may contain fishmeal, but these are usually for ornamentals rather than domestic breeds. Egg and table breeds are best fed on a free-range or organic ration that has plant-sourced proteins. This caters for consumer preference, as well as ensuring that eggs do not acquire a fishy taste.

It is important to remember that the nutritional requirements vary at different stages. Ducklings require a higher percentage of protein than adults, so a starter ration of compound crumbs is advisable. These are available without anti-coccidiostat medications which some chick crumb rations contain. A starter ration is usually given for the first few weeks of life.

There are also grower rations for young ducks, to follow on after the starter crumbs. This type of feed has a reduced level of protein, normally around 15%, but may be even lower if slow-growing, free-range table ducks are being reared.

Before the breeding season starts, it is a good idea to feed a breeder ration to domestic and ornamental breeds. This formulation ensures that the breeding birds are not lacking in any of the crucial nutrients, and the ducklings are less likely to suffer from nutritional deficiency complaints.

Feeders need to be heavy-based otherwise the ducks will soon tip them over. Here, the ducks are being given their daily compound feed in such a feeder, but their afternoon grain is given to them on the ground. (See page 4).

Most ducks will forage for 'extras' in grassland or pond margins. See the duck on the outside front cover whose muddy bill testifies to her expertise in browsing.

Examples of Compound Rations for Ducks

Duck Starter Crumbs
(From hatch to 2-6 weeks)
Protein: 19%
Oil: 4.50%
Fibre: 4.50%

Duck Breeder Pellets
(For breeding ducks)
Protein: 16%
Oil: 4.50%
Fibre: 6.50%

Laying Ration for Ducks
(From point of lay)
Protein: 17%
Oil: 3.5%
Fibre: 6.4%

Duck Grower/Finisher Pellets
(After starter ration)
Protein: 15%
Oil: 3.25%
Fibre: 7%

Ornamental Duck Pellets *
(General maintenance feed)
Protein: 16%
Oil: 3%
Fibre: 7%

* The formulation varies according to the type of ducks. Some are also made to float on water for sea ducks such as Eiders, Goldeneyes, Mergansers and Smews.

Ducks will also take free-range layer's pellets of the kind formulated for chickens. They are suitable for all types of ducks, not just the egg producers, and may indeed be the only type of feed available in some smaller feed stockist shops.

The morning when the ducks are released from their house is a good time to give a compound feed. Placing the pellets in a shallow, heavy-based feeder prevents them from being wasted by being trampled upon and dispersed into a mush.

Where ornamentals are concerned, compound feeds formulated specifically for them are available from some feed suppliers. (They will also take poultry layer's pellets as described above). Some ornamental feed pellets are made to float on the surface of the water. These are particularly appropriate for sea ducks, such as Eiders, Goldeneyes, Mergansers and Smews, that need a higher protein feed to make up for the lack of fish which they would normally catch.

Natural and organic compound feeds are available, as distinct from the normal rations that are produced for the intensive sector. They are free of artificial additives, antibiotics or egg yolk colouring agents, a particularly important aspect for those keeping egg layers or rearing table ducks. It is also important not to give grower feeds such as those formulated for turkeys, or those produced for the intensive sector generally, because some of the additives in them are toxic to ducks. These feeds are also much higher in protein than is necessary, even for insectivorous ducks. Turkey feeds, for example, may be as high as 24% protein. Too high a level can result in an accelerated rate of growth, so that weak leg or slipped wing problems may develop. There is a list of specialist feed suppliers in the reference section. Examples of compound feeds that are available are shown in the table above.

Grain

Grain such as wheat or a mixed grain ration is popular with ducks, both domestic and ornamental breeds. It is useful to feed it in the afternoon, particularly when placed on a clean area of ground. Unlike pellets, the grains will not disintegrate into a mush and are soon scooped up.

The domestic duck's bill is adapted for scooping up its food. Some powdered or mash feeds may clog the nostrils. Water nearby is essential.

Ornamentals in larger collections are often given their grain ration in shallow water. This helps to deter wild birds, such as pigeons and starlings, from helping themselves. A long, shallow and perforated trough or dish will keep the grain in one place, in shallow water near the bank, while preventing it from becoming submerged in mud. Alternatively, the grain can be fed in a shallow, non-perforated trough on land, with a little fresh water on top. Where domestic ducklings are being introduced to whole grains for the first time, it is a good idea to soften them in water first, until they get used to it. As they get older, they soon get used to eating it dry, but it is important that their drinker is always close by. Small breeds may prefer to have kibbled (chopped) grains.

Wheat is, in many ways, the best all-round grain for ducks. Good quality wheat is approximately 11% protein. Oats are high in oils as well as protein and are therefore a useful winter feed. They are not always popular on their own however, and may need to be mixed in with wheat. In summer, the heat-producing qualities may be too great and it is wise to reduce the amount, or not to feed them at all, unless they are in a mixed grain ration from suppliers. Maize is also high in oils and is usually a constituent of mixed grain. Barley is a useful source of nutrients, but again, on its own will tend to be left. The source of barley is also important because some of the chemical sprays used on the plants in some arable areas may be toxic to poultry. A letter from a friend in the USA detailed how she had lost some chickens in this way.

Our practice, when it came to feeding grain, was to feed wheat in the summer months and mixed grain from a feed supplier in winter. The extra calories helped to compensate for the additional demands made on the system during the cold months.

Poultry grit and crushed oystershell

It is important to make fine poultry grit available, particularly where whole grains are given. It keeps the gizzard functioning normally, allowing the grit to act as small millstones to grind up the grains. Free-ranging ducks will often find their own source of grit.

Crushed oystershell is also recommended in the diet, especially for egg producers and for those which are kept as breeding birds. It helps to ensure that sufficient levels of calcium are available for strong egg shells. Most feed stockists will sell both poultry grit and crushed oystershell. They can be placed in a shallow container and left under cover so that the ducks can help themselves as required.

Grazing and greens

Most ducks will forage on grass and marginal areas, but some, such as the Wigeon and Muscovy have a definite need to graze. Areas of pasture will therefore need to be made available if these breeds are kept. Short-growing grasses are preferable to longer ones, and it may be necessary to mow the pasture to keep it short, as well as to produce new, fresh growth. If a grassed area is to be sown, a suitable mixture would contain Perennial Ryegrass, Cocksfoot, Timothy, Fescues and White Clover.

Other greens that ducks are particularly fond of are Chickweed, *Stellaria media*, and vegetable garden greens such as lettuce and cabbage. They will often eat plants *in situ* where they are growing in patches, but if picked for them they should be shredded into small pieces to prevent digestive blockages. Alternatively, bunches can be suspended in an enclosure. It is easy to cause an imbalance in the diet by too much feeding of one thing at the expense of another. Our practice was to let the ducks browse for greens themselves, so that they were only taking 'standing' plants. This was foraging in the field, with access to the vegetable garden in winter, when they did a useful job of weed clearance and pest control for us. Their basic diet, however, was compound pellets and grain.

Pond feeding

Pond plants such as the floating duckweed, *Lemna minor*, are a valuable source of food for dabbling ducks. Other plants provide oxygen in the water as well as a habitat for insect larvae. These, in turn may be eaten, as well as fish and even the occasional frog. Reference has already been made to floating compound pellets that are available for ornamentals, such as the Mergansers, as well as to the practice of placing grain in perforated troughs in the water for ornamentals in general.

Feeding practice

Our practice, which always worked well, was to give a compound ration of pellets in the morning, when the ducks were first let out of their house. The pellets were placed in a long, wide and heavy based feeder that they could not tip over.

Ducks' bills are adapted for scooping so that the bill goes into and under the food. It is important to avoid powdery foods otherwise the nostrils can become clogged. If a compound mash (powder) ration is given rather than a pelleted feed, it should be moistened with water in order to produce a crumb consistency. This can also clog the nostrils however, and I prefer to give pellets so that this problem does not occur. The feeder also stays cleaner, an important aspect in preventing disease. All feeders should, of course, be cleaned on a regular basis. Whatever form the food is in, there should be fresh water nearby. Domestic ducks will often eat some food, then waddle over to the drinker before returning for some more food. Having the feeder and drinker close to each other therefore makes sense. In a run, it is a good idea to have these placed on a slatted area so that water falls through, otherwise there will soon be a marsh.

As soon as our ducks had eaten, they would rush off to the pond, spending the rest of the day dabbling about there, and browsing on the grass and in the hedges. In the afternoon, they were given their grain ration on the grass. More pond dabbling and browsing would ensue until dusk when they went into their house for the night. If ducks are reluctant to go in, a little bit of grain in the house soon makes them change their minds. Once they are going in, however, it is as well to discontinue the practice, in case rats are attracted to the house and gnaw their way in.

Drinker on slatted area allowing spills to fall through preventing boggy conditions.

There are obviously many different feeding regimes, depending on the type of ducks and nature of the enterprise but as a general rule, the guidelines are:

Ducklings (hatch to 2-3 weeks)	Duck starter crumbs
Table ducks (2-3 weeks to slaughter)	Grower pellets and grain
Laying ducks (2-3 weeks to point of lay)	Grower pellets and grain
Laying ducks (point of lay onwards)	Layer's pellets and grain
Adult breeding ducks	Layer's pellets and grain (or mixed grain only) most of the year Breeder's ration late autumn to winter
Ornamental ducklings	Duck starter crumbs as above
Young ornamental ducks	Grower pellets and grain (or grain only)
Adult ornamental ducks	Ornamental duck pellets and grain depending on breed.

Home feeds

Home-produced feed can be given, as long as it does not provide too much of one thing at the expense of other nutrients, as referred to earlier. Suitable ingredients include green or vegetable garden foods such as nettles, lettuce, carrots, brassicas and alfalfa (lucerne), etc. They should be well chopped or shredded so that there are no items large enough to cause impaction. They must be used fresh, with any leftovers disposed of before they become mouldy. (The latter is a sure way of introducing disease). Boiled potatoes (not green) mixed to a crumb consistency with wheatmeal or oatmeal is a good ration for table ducks, especially with chopped greens added. Whole mixed grain is also appreciated with this ration..

Fresh, salt-free kitchen scraps are fine for the household flock, but should not be given where table ducks or eggs are sold.

The correct way to carry a duck is to support it from below while confining the wings to stop flapping.

Ducks will usually use nest boxes that are provided for them, as long as they are not placed in inaccessible positions. The nesting material needs to be changed frequently where domestic ducks are kept for egg production so that the eggs are kept clean.

Egg cartons and descriptive labels are available for packaging and selling duck eggs.

Eggs

An egg boiled very soft is not unwholesome.
(Emma - Jane Austen)

There are all sorts of myths about duck eggs, the most prevalent being that they carry salmonella and will inevitably cause food poisoning. This dates back to the period after World War II, when a report on salmonella listed the foods that carried salmonella risks. At that time there were still many commercial duck farms in existence, and when duck eggs were included in the list, it produced such a consumer reaction against them that virtually all the duck farms went out of existence. This was despite the fact that duck eggs came quite low down in the list, with cooked meats and ice cream being the main culprits.

We now know that salmonella can exist in *all* eggs, whether they be chicken, duck or any other kind of egg, or whether they are battery, free-range or organically produced. The advice with *all* eggs is that pregnant women, children, the old and the sick should only eat eggs that have been hard-boiled, despite what Jane Austen claimed in the quotation above. Strenuous efforts have been made in recent years to flock-test and to ensure that the risks of salmonella are kept to an absolute minimum. If buying in layers, check with the supplier that they are from a samonella-tested flock.

Duck eggs do have larger pores than the shells of chicken eggs, but provided they are laid in clean conditions, collected regularly and stored in cool, clean conditions, they are just as safe to eat as chicken eggs. It is nice to see that duck eggs are becoming more widely available again. The pack shown on the left was bought in my local supermarket.

Nutritional value

Duck eggs are larger than hen's eggs (See the photograph on page 44 for comparison). They contain more protein and fat than a hen's egg, but less water. Typical food values are as follows:

Per egg - Energy: 108kcal (449kJ). Protein: 9.4g. Fat: 7.3g. Carbohydrate: Trace
Per 100g - Energy: 163kcal (680kJ). Protein: 14.3g. Fat: 11.8g. Carbohydrate: Trace.

Their larger size also means that cooking times for boiling need to be longer than they are for chicken eggs. They are as follows: Soft-boiled - 4 minutes and 45 seconds. Firm white and soft yolk - 8 minutes. Hard-boiled: 13 minutes.

The eggs of free-ranging ducks often have deep yellow yolks from their grazing activities. This is particularly true of Muscovy eggs because they tend to graze on grass more than other domestic breeds. Duck eggs can, of course, be used for any purpose that chicken eggs are used for, as long as they are regarded as equivalent to large sized hen eggs, rather than medium or small.

Egg laying

An egg starts off in the duck's ovary, then is released into the oviduct. As it travels down, it is first coated with membranes and then receives the shell coating from the shell gland, before being laid. The whole process takes between 24 - 36 hours.

Domestic ducks come into lay at 21-26 weeks of age. Commercial strains have been bred to commence laying earlier than non-commercial breeds. If egg numbers are the priority, then it makes sense to choose one of the commercial strains indicated on pages 53-54. The Khaki Campbell has a long record of being the prime egg layer, easily outlaying chickens. The Kortlang strain can produce up to 350 eggs.

Low access nesting areas should be made available for laying ducks, and the nesting material changed frequently in order to keep the eggs clean. They should be collected frequently, then stored in cool conditions where the temperature can be maintained at around 10-12°C .

It is often said that ducks will not use nest boxes and lay their eggs anywhere. As with most things, 'the truth lies somewhere in between'. As referred to earlier, nest boxes that are positioned low down, without a high step-over access are much more likely to be used. Most of our ducks got into the habit of using them, especially after we had put some pot eggs in the nest boxes to encourage them. There were always a few floor-laid eggs, of course, but then no-one's perfect! Our problem initially was that of letting the ducks out too early. They would make a quick dash for the pond so that eggs were laid on the grass, on the bank or even in the water. The magpies would swoop down to enjoy the feast. Letting the ducks out later in the morning did the trick.

The onset of lay obviously commences when sexual maturity is reached, but there are other factors involved, such as the time of year. The eyes and head area are receptive to light. As the day length increases, the ovary is stimulated into action. Temperature also affects the egg-laying system. Cold, late springs may delay things.

It is often claimed that the onset of lay can be recognised by the 'dropping' of the keel or abdomen in the female, but this is not necessarily the case, particularly in first-time layers. Older ducks tend to have a lower abdomen anyway, whether they are laying or not. Head nodding action between a male and female is a sure indication that egg laying is imminent or has already started. Although domestic ducks are generally better at winter laying than chickens, they may still need some extra light to encourage them into laying. This is not difficult to arrange and involves providing a light bulb and time switch in the duck house. No more than a total of 15 hours of light (combined daylight and artificial) should be given on humanitarian grounds.

Feeding layers

Laying ducks will do very well on a compound duck laying ration which contains 17% protein, 3.5% oil and 6.4% fibre. A compound, free-range or organic chicken feed ration is also suitable. It is difficult to be precise, but on average, one laying duck will need around 150g of pellets a day. This obviously depends on the age and level of production of the bird, with more being given for high producers. A perhaps simpler method of estimating quantities is to give enough pellets that the ducks will consume within 20 minutes. The pellets can be given in the morning when the ducks are let out. During the day, they can then forage on pasture and dabble in their pond.

Grain such as wheat can be given in the afternoon before the ducks are put back in their house. On average, around 25g per bird, per day, is adequate, although the amount should be increased in winter to cater for the extra demand on the metabolism of keeping warm as well as laying. Again, a total amount that the ducks will all consume within 20 minutes is a fair estimate of quantity. It goes without saying that drinking water should be available in drinkers close to the feeding area. If placed on a slatted base or moved regularly, there is less likelihood of the area becoming muddy.

Poultry grit should be made available for the gizzard to function properly, as well as some crushed oystershell to ensure that sufficient calcium levels are available for good egg shell production. These can both be put in a container, under cover, to which the ducks have regular access, so that they can help themselves as necessary.

Selling eggs

On a small scale, selling eggs at the farmgate, farm shop or market stall is probably the best option. The eggs are not graded according to size and it is not necessary to be registered as a producer, although obviously all food safety precautions should be taken. No dirty, washed or cracked eggs should be sold. These can be hard-boiled and used in the home, as long as they are fresh.

On a large scale, duck eggs are often sold through a registered packer or distributor who arranges for the collection, packaging and sale of the eggs. It requires regular supplies on the part of the producer but there is little control of the price, for this will be determined by the distributor working within the retail chain.

Egg cartons such as those used for chicken eggs are suitable for duck eggs. They are available in varying quantities from specialist packaging suppliers. Descriptive labels are also available. Both cartons and labels can be pre-printed with the producer's details, as required. The carton illustrated on page 68, for example, has the name of the farm, the fact that the six eggs are free-range and also represent *'a taste of luxury'*. There is a 'Best before' date and advice to keep the eggs refrigerated after purchase. The name and address of the distributor are on the back of the carton, along with an identifying barcode. Inside the carton lid the following information is provided for consumers:

" Church & Manor Duck eggs are a natural product full of richness and flavour. Ideal for that luxury weekend breakfast and delicious in any egg recipe. They are produced to the highest hygiene and welfare standards. Small flocks of ducks spend their day in grassy paddocks and their nights in the shelter of well-ventilated barns with fresh straw bedding. Their high quality food is produced at our own mill and excludes any GM crops or artificial yolk colorants. ' (Manor Farms & Deans Foods Ltd)

Structure of the egg

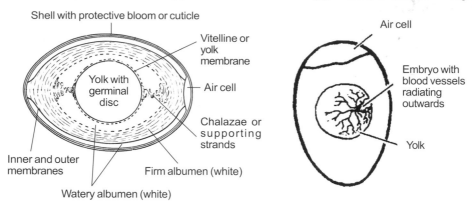

Shell with protective bloom or cuticle

Vitelline or yolk membrane

Yolk with germinal disc

Air cell

Chalazae or supporting strands

Inner and outer membranes

Firm albumen (white)

Watery albumen (white)

Fertile egg when candled at 7 days

Air cell

Embryo with blood vessels radiating outwards

Yolk

Correct size of air cell in relation to incubation time

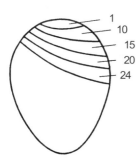

1
10
15
20
24

Checking the size of the air cell at the appropriate number of days is an accurate way of determining whether the correct amount of water is being lost from the egg. If it is too big, the humidity is too low and should be increased. If too small, the humidity is too high and should be decreased.

Another method of checking the relative humidity is to weigh a few samples from each batch of eggs. Over the course of incubation, up to pipping stage, a duck egg needs to lose 11-13% of its weight

Rearing pen for the first week

Heat lamp placed above the pen

Droppings fall through so there is less likelihood of disease

Flat weldmesh panels make up the floor of the pen which is in a barn or shed.

Broody coop for mother and ducklings

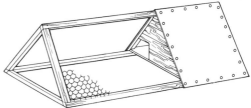

Once the ducklings have hatched, the coop needs to be moved regularly so that it is always on clean ground, unused by other waterfowl or poultry.

Once the ducks are independent, they can be transferred to a housing system such as the ones shown on pages 30 and 80, depending on the enterprise.

Breeding

Strain is more important than breed.

To breed replacement ducks it is necessary to start with good breeding birds. They need to be healthy, vigorous and good examples of their type. The male and female should not be too closely related, otherwise the chance of congenital defects in the young is increased. An exception to this rule is where a particularly good trait is required. A good male, for example, could be mated to one of his daughters if she had the same characteristic, while a female could be crossed with one of her sons. Within the European Union there is a requirement for those with a breeding flock of 250 birds or more to be registered and to flock-test their breeders for salmonella. (Further information is available from DEFRA).

A good balanced diet for the breeding birds is essential, for a deficiency of some nutrients may show up as defects in the ducklings. It is a good idea therefore to give them a purpose made breeder's ration rather than a grower's or a layer's ration.

If a specific mating is required, pen the birds in the same enclosure. If the females have previously been running with different males, it will be necessary to discard their eggs for at least three weeks, for this is the length of time that sperms can remain viable in the oviduct. As a general rule, heavy breeds of domestic ducks would have a mating ratio of no more than seven ducks to one drake. Light breeds could be one drake to a maximum of ten ducks. This is a generalisation, for there are always exceptions. The heavyweights such as Aylesbury and Rouen, for example, might be one drake to two ducks. Pure breeds might only be required in small numbers, so pairs would be appropriate. Some ornamental ducks bond for life, so pairs are also needed here. Call ducks are usually in pairs or trios. The best females to select for breeding are two year olds. Their eggs will be a good size and the first year will have been a time for observation and recording before selection for breeding takes place. The same applies to drakes. They are both at their best for breeding purposes, up to the age of four years, although individual birds may prove to be viable breeders for longer than this. Keeping records is vital and identification of the breeds by means of leg rings allows this to take place. Leg rings can be of different colours or have unique numbers on them.

The question is frequently asked - is it necessary to have a pond for mating to take place? The point has been made earlier that ducks are waterfowl and are at their most content in their natural medium, but they will mate on land as well as on water. Where water does become essential is for heavy breeds such as the show Aylesbury and Rouen which are literally too cumbersome to mate on land. The drakes of most species are more highly coloured than the females, providing for display before mating takes place. There is also a great deal of chasing and flapping along the surface of ponds at this time, while head nodding between the sexes is a sure indication that mating is about to take place.

Natural incubation

Many breeds of ornamental ducks will make nests and incubate their eggs, if conditions are right. This includes having the right degree of shelter, and the correct type of nestbox, placed at the appropriate height. Some are ground layers, while others prefer nestboxes that are partially underground. Some require them to be above ground. (See the table on pages 58-59 for further information).

Domestic ducks are not generally regarded as good mothers, although in my experience, they are better from their second year. Even some of my Khaki Campbells acquitted themselves well, but refused to consider making nests anywhere other than under the hedge in the field. Egg laying in specific and protected areas can be encouraged by placing 'pot' eggs in the nests. Bear in mind that corvids such as magpies and rooks may steal the eggs from unprotected nests. Making a 'tent' structure over the nest is a good idea if the duck cannot be moved to nest elsewhere. A broody duck will sit tight on her nest, hissing at anyone who tries to disturb her. She is less likely to be put off if she is reasonably tame. It is important that she has protection from predators and external parasites, and that food and water are available close by.

Broody hens can also be used to hatch duck eggs, although they need to be reliable sitters that will not give up before the hatching period. (A chicken's egg takes 21 days, while that of most domestic ducks is 28 days). The other drawback with using hens is that they are not able to preen the ducklings before their preen glands are functioning properly, so the ducklings need to be kept off water for the first few weeks. Small bantam breeds of chickens are particularly good as broodies, and are often used for hatching Call duck eggs, as well as those of ornamentals. (See the photograph on page 49). The Muscovy duck is also renowned for her motherly capabilities but is more appropriate for incubating the eggs of the larger breeds. Small ducklings are more likely to become lost or inadvertently squashed.

Artificial incubation

Broody hens are not always available so it may be appropriate to consider using an incubator. Fertile eggs can be removed from a nest and stored for about a week before they are put in the incubator. Store them, broad end up, in egg cartons at a temperature of 15 - 18°C. Before putting them in the incubator, allow them to come up to room temperature so that there is not too abrupt a temperature change. Eggs that are older than a week may still hatch, but hatchability declines at the rate of 2% a day after the first two days.

There are many incubators available, but the modern ones are more precise and less labour intensive to use than older models. Ideally, they should be well insulated and have an automatic egg turning facility (otherwise you will have to turn the eggs by hand several times a day). They may be 'still air' or 'fan assisted' where air is driven through by means of a fan. The provision of adequate ventilation to provide oxygen and take away carbon dioxide is obviously crucial.

Washing eggs in warm water and an egg sanitant before putting them in the incubator helps to reduce the chances of infection killing the embryo.

Temperature is controlled by means of a thermostat, while a humidity gauge is used to indicate the relative humidity of the air. (Comprehensive details of both natural and artificial incubation, including choosing, making and using incubators, are given in the book *Incubation - A Guide to Hatching and Rearing*).

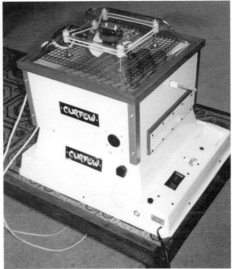
A tabletop incubator used by the author. It has a fan on top and a dehumidifier at the bottom. The thermometer can be seen on the right.

Select only clean, undamaged eggs that are of medium size, for they are less likely to encounter problems. Large ones, for example may be double-yolked.They should be free of hairline cracks and have even, unblemished shells. Before they are placed in the incubator they should be washed in hot water that is comfortable to the hand and which has had an egg sanitant added to it. This is available from incubator suppliers, or a product such as that used for sterilizing baby bottles is suitable. Egg washing helps to ensure that disease organisms that might otherwise kill the developing embryo are kept to a minimum.

Clean and sterilize the incubator then run it for 24 hours before use, to make sure that it is working satisfactorily. Place it in a room in the house rather than in a shed outside. Many people do not realise that the temperature *outside* the incubator is almost as important as that inside, and helps to make the controlling of humidity an easier proposition.The optimum conditions at the centre of each egg are as follows:

Domestic ducks: Temperature 37.5⁰C for days 1-25
                              37⁰C for days 26-28
              Humidity 58% for days 1-25
                          75% for days 26-28

Muscovy ducks: Temperature 37.5⁰C for days 1-31
                              37⁰C for days 32-34
              Humidity 60% for days 1-31
                          75% for days 32-34

Ornamental ducks: Temperature 37.5⁰C for days 1- pipping stage *
                              37⁰C for pipping to hatch *

* Incubation periods vary depending on the breed. The first or pipping stage may be from 19-27 days, while the second or hatching period may be at 22-30 days. See chart on pages 58-59.

Above: A polypropylene weeding bag for a small number of ducklings. Wood shavings are used after the first few days, when there is no longer any danger of the ducklings eating them. Starter crumbs are placed in an egg carton and the small drinker ensures that they can drink without getting wet.

Inspecting the ducklings in a purpose-made brooder.

Candling can take place 5-7 days after incubation starts. This is where each egg is held against a bright light so that the contents can be seen. The developing embryo can be seen as a red 'starfish' shape. Any infertile or 'clear' eggs can be discarded. Candlers are available from incubator suppliers or you can make your own using a torch in a box with a hole in it, or a cardboard tube placed around the torch. Candlers are also useful for checking eggs for hairline cracks before incubation, as well as checking that the right amount of water is being lost from the egg during incubation. This is indicated by the size of the air cell that supplies the developing embryo with oxygen while removing carbon dioxide. The correct size of the air cell during stages of the incubation period is shown in the diagram on page 72.

The 'pipping' stage is when the duckling is ready to break through the shell. At this stage, turning of the eggs ceases, the temperature is reduced slightly and the humidity increased. It is vital to follow the instructions that come with individual incubators for they may vary in how they achieve this. Some larger breeders, use separate incubators and hatchers for the two stages.

Once the ducklings begin to break through the shell, they should ideally be left undisturbed. Only when it is obvious that nothing is happening for a long period should any 'help' be given. This involves dampening the shell with a damp cloth and carefully unpicking the shell. Stop immediately if bleeding occurs and try later.

Rearing

Once out of their shells, the ducklings should be left for 24 hours, to allow them to dry out and fluff up their down feathers. They still have the remnants of the egg yolk in their abdomen, so will not need feeding at this time. After 24 hours they can be moved to a brooder - a secure area with a heat lamp about 50cm (20in) above it, to keep them warm. The height of the heater can be adjusted according to the behaviour of the ducklings. If clustered in a tight ball, they are too cold so the lamp needs lowering; if widely dispersed to the edges, they are too hot, so it should be raised.

A brooder can be anything from a large cardboard box to a section of an outside shed. There are also purpose-made ones available. For small numbers, I have found a polypropylene weeding bag to be ideal. With a thick layer of fabric (such as pieces of old sheet) to provide a non-slip floor, it is also easy to keep clean and to lift. Non-slip surfaces are important in order to avoid splayed legs. After a day or two, when the ducklings are eating properly, they are provided with

Two-week old duckling. At this stage it is ready to face the outside world, but still needs night-time warmth and protection.

wood shavings instead of the fabric. For the first few days, I avoid these in case they try and eat them. Sawdust should also be avoided as it can clog up the nostrils.

Whatever the scale, it is essential to provide warmth, ventilation, a predator proof area and a non-slip floor. Many commercial breeders use pens with weldmesh floors for the first week so that the droppings fall through, lessening the possibility of disease. (See page 72). After a week, the ducklings are allowed out into a protected barn area with wood shavings or dust-free chopped straw (which is cheaper) as litter. This will need to be added to and replenished on a regular basis. Raking it through will also help to introduce air and keep it dry. Disease pathogens are thus deterred.

A duck starter crumb ration is ideal for the young birds for the first couple of weeks, with drinking water provided in a drinker that does not allow them to climb in. If their down feathers become wet and spiky, they may invite pecking and bullying from the others. The feed crumbs and drinking water should be available at all times, so that they can help themselves as needed. As they grow, they can be switched gradually to a rearing ration, and grain can also be introduced. The latter can be soaked to soften it, to get them used to taking it. As they get older, they often learn to take it dry. (See page 65 for information on feeding grain to ornamental ducks). As with all dietary changes or additions, it should be a gradual process of introduction.

Ducklings grow quickly, and the sooner they are able to excercise and go outside, the better for their growth and development. If the weather is not too harsh, they should be able to go out from the age of 2 - 3 weeks. A small house with a covered run is ideal, for they may be at risk from overhead predators. Hawks have been known to take Call ducklings, for example.

One of the drawbacks of artificial incubation, it must be said, is that ducklings tend to regard the first moving thing as 'mother'. If this happens to be you, you will become imprinted as 'mum' and it may not be convenient to be accompanied by a flock of ducklings. Broody hens are not able to preen ducklings to make them waterproof. Incubator-hatched ducklings are similarly at risk. Until the preen glands function fully, they must be kept away from swimming water. It is also worth remembering that Muscovy ducklings, and those of other wood ducks, are able to climb. An open-roofed brooder will therefore need some netting over it to confine them.

Sexing ducklings

It is possible to tell the sex of a duckling by various means before it becomes obvious, but the earlier the age, the more difficult it is.

• **Autosexing** This is where a male and female of the same breed are crossed, and the down colour of the ducklings differs according to whether they are males or females. For example, when a Khaki Campbell male is crossed with a Dark Khaki female, the male ducklings will be dark brown, while the females are lighter. The cross does not work the other way around.

• **Sex linkage** This is when a male and female of different breeds are crossed, and produce ducklings whose sex can be indicated by the down feather colouring or markings. For example, when a genetically brown coloured drake is crossed with genetically black or grey females, the coloured areas of the down will be black or grey in the male ducklings and brown in the females. Again, the cross does not work the other way around.

Genetically brown males include: Khaki Campbell, Chocolate Indian Runner, and Chocolate Muscovy. Genetically black or grey females include Dark Campbell, Cayuga, Black Indian Runner, Silver Appleyard, and Black Muscovy,

• **Vent sexing** This should not be attempted without having first had the technique demonstrated by someone experienced, for it is easy to damage the duckling. Hold the duckling gently, head downwards, so that the vent is between the thumb and forefinger. Gently press the second finger which is behind the bird's back, and at the same time, push the forefinger back slightly so that the vent is exposed. Now, with the other hand, hold the vent on each side with the thumb and forefinger and press down slightly in order to open the vent. In the male, the penis will be seen as a tiny projectile. It will be necessary to check several ducklings before the distinction is clear, but once achieved, sexing becomes a relatively easy technique.

• **Tail feathers** In the domestic breeds (apart from the Muscovy) the curling tail feathers or sex curls become apparent at a few weeks of age.

• **Bill colour** With some pure breeds, there is a colour difference in the bills that begins to show from around six weeks. For example, the Call and Rouen drake both begin to show a greenish bill, while that of the female is orange-brown. In other pure breeds, the female's bill is generally darker than that of the male.

• **Different voice** Again, as the ducklings of the domestic breeds grow, the females have a definite 'quack' while the males have what might be described as a 'half-quack' or a muted squeak. This difference begins to become apparent from around 5 weeks onwards.

Once the ducklings are sexed, it is a good idea to give them identifying marks such as a colour-coded or numbered leg ring, if they are to become future breeding stock.

Table ducks

Choose ducks with plump bellies, and with thick
and yellowish feet. (Mrs Beeton, 1859)

In Britain, the traditional table duck was the Aylesbury, and thousands were pro-
duced and sent by train to destinations all over Britain, but particularly to London.
Eventually, however, its keel counted against it as far as poulterers were concerned.
The Pekin was crossed with the Aylesbury to produce a bird with less keel, but with a
good growth rate. These days, commercial strains of table ducks are available. In
Britain, the best known table strains based on the Pekin/Aylesbury cross are from
Cherry Valley. There are also commercial strains based on the Muscovy that are avail-
able from France. Reference has already been made to the Gressingham duck that
was based on the wild Mallard for an increased 'gamey' flavour.

If a table duck enterprise is envisaged, it is possible to concentrate on a commercial strain, or on a utility strain of pure breed and possibly produce your own crosses.
Reference was made earlier to the Whalesbury hybrid that was the result of crossing
the Welsh Harlequin with the Aylesbury. We found that when killed at 9-10 weeks,
these provided an oven-ready bird of about 1.1kg (2.5lb). When raised to 16 - 20
weeks, they gave an oven-ready weight of around 1.8kg (4lb). Commercial strains
will produce heavier birds, of around 3.6kg (8b) in a relatively short growing period,
sometimes even as short as seven weeks. Details of commercial table breeds are listed
on pages 53-54.

Duck meat

Duck meat is higher in fat than that of chickens, although it is less so in ducks that
have been reared on free-range and given a less intensive diet than that provided for
indoor-reared ones. The combination of a less intensive ration and outdoor exercise
means that the ducks gain weight more slowly. The aim with many intensively reared
ones is to get them to killing weight in the shortest possible time, and this inevitably
produces fattier meat that is relatively bland to the taste. Small table duck enterprises
that have a more natural and humane approach, such as those recommended by the
RSPCA's *Freedom Food* programme or the Soil Association's *Organic Standards*,
will produce ducks with leaner meat and a better flavour. These factors, together with
the welfare considerations, provide excellent selling points. Local Farmer's Markets
are also increasing in popularity, providing the small producer with ready outlets.

It is also worth mentioning that some commercial Pekin and Aylesbury strains
tend to have more fatty meat than breeds such as the Muscovy and Saxony, or the
lightweight and bantam breeds.These are all naturally lower in body fat and when
raised in non-intensive conditions, their meat is similar to that of wild ducks in lean-
ness and flavour.

Two methods of rearing table ducks on a small scale

Perimeter fence at least 2m high or protected by electric fencing

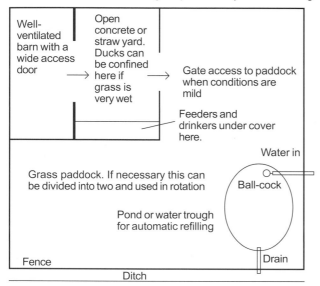

Well-ventilated barn with a wide access door

Open concrete or straw yard. Ducks can be confined here if grass is very wet

Gate access to paddock when conditions are mild

Feeders and drinkers under cover here.

Grass paddock. If necessary this can be divided into two and used in rotation

Water in

Ball-cock

Pond or water trough for automatic refilling

Fence

Drain

Ditch

This system has a barn or shed facing away from the prevailing winds, but with good ventilation. The floor inside is covered with dry litter such as chopped straw that is regularly raked and replaced as necessary.

An open concrete or straw yard provides exercise when the grass is unavailable or being rested. At one end of this is a covered area for feeders and drinkers.

This system is also suitable for an egg-laying flock, particularly if a bank of low access nest boxes is made available in the barn.

Shed with access to running water

Water in

Wide access doors to concrete ramp and water

Also fenced here

Next shed here, fenced off from first shed and from that section of water, so batches of ducks are kept separate.

Water out

This system could be used where a paddock is not available, but where running water is easy to provide or divert as a stream.

If required, a series of sheds can be placed end to end, and each one, together with its section of stream, is fenced off from the others.

On a smaller scale, this system could also be used for a breeding enterprise, where it is necessary to keep different breeds separate, to avoid inter-breeding.

(See also the photograph on page 44 that shows a commercial house with water flowing through it).

Table ducks being reared in a shed with chopped straw on the ground. Most commercial rearers do not let the ducks out, but small producers allow them access to grass range. (*Kidd Farm machinery*)

Housing

It must be said that most table ducks are reared intensively, in large barns with no access to the outside world, and with access to drinking water only. This is abhorrent for birds that are naturally adapted to water. The small-scale enterprise is far better advised to cater for the free-range or organic markets, concentrating on local sales.

Any well-ventilated barn or shed can be used for free-range table ducks. If there is also access to a grass ranging area, this is even better. If not, a concrete yard or outside strawed area can be made available for exercise. (It is worth mentioning that a straw yard is really only feasible in drier areas of the country, or in particularly dry periods of the year). Polytunnels with netted ventilation panels are also popular as housing in pasture land.

A pond, trough or series of troughs with automatic watering will provide water for immersing the head, splashing the feathers or even allowing dabbling to take place. A ball-cock will allow the water level to adjust automatically, while a drain facility will take away surplus water when the tank is being cleaned. As referred to earlier, it is necessary to get permission from the Environment Agency if natural streams or watercourses are dammed or diverted to provide ponds. Where water is draining into a ditch or water course, it is important to ensure that it does not go onto anyone else's land, and that it does not cause nitrogen pollution from the droppings.

The shed floor should be kept well covered and replenished as required, so that it is always dry. Chopped straw or wood shavings are used, although the former is cheaper. Whole straw should be avoided because it matts very easily and is difficult to handle when it gets wet. Chopped straw can be raked easily so that air is introduced into the litter layer. This has the double effect of keeping it dry and ensuring that disease pathogens do not gain a hold in damp areas.

Feeding and rearing

Ducklings can either be bought in as day-olds, or they may have been reared on site. For the first week they will require to be kept in heated pens, as shown on page 72. After this, they are ready to be introduced to their barn or shed. If the heated pens are *in situ*, this will simply be a matter of opening them into the remaining area of the barn so that there is no stress associated with a move. If the weather is mild, the ducklings can be allowed out as soon as possible into their exercise yard. From here, they can then progress to a grass area, if one is available. It goes without saying that ducks need to be protected against rats in their house, and against foxes and other predators in their run or paddock.

A duck starter ration of compound crumbs is ideal for the ducklings. This is also available as an organic ration, and together with water, meets all their nutritional requirements at this stage. It is important not to let the ducklings have access to dabbling water until they have lost their baby down. Their preen glands do not function properly at this stage, and in the absence of a mother duck which would normally preen them, they will become waterlogged and chilled. Drinkers that they can drink from without being able to climb into are ideal.

The ducklings can gradually go over to a duck grower ration as they develop. Again, a free-range or organic formulation is best. This can be given in the mornings, with wheat in the afternoons. If they have access to grass, they will also benefit from their browsing activities. Where grain is given, the ducks should have access to a container of poultry grit from where they can help themselves.

Home-produced feeds can be produced if the rearer has mixing facilities, and the ingredients are home-grown or available locally at a reasonable price. The greater the quantity, the cheaper the price, but bulk purchases also require adequate storage facilities. Grains can be ground up in a small home mill and then mixed together as required. They should be used as soon as possible in order to retain the optimum nutritional value. I know one producer who bought a new, small concrete mixer, and used it just for mixing duck feeds. The result will be a 'mix' of course, rather than compound pellets. A suitable mixture would be as follows, although there are many variations, depending upon what ingredients are available.

> 4 parts wheat meal: 3 parts barley meal: 2 parts ground oats: 1 part maize meal
> Trace of vitamin and mineral supplement or a little brewer's yeast

Skim milk and cooked potatoes have also been used for table ducks, but care should be taken to ensure that too much of any one ingredient at the expense of others is avoided, for it is easy to cause a nutritional imbalance. Where feeds are mixed with water or skimmed milk to provide a mash feed, there is also a greater risk of digestive upsets. The feed must be fresh, while the feeders are cleaned regularly. Where table ducks are to be sold, rather than produced for the home, it is advisable to use a good quality proprietary ration that has been formulated for free-range or organic use.

Slaughtering and processing

Depending upon the breed or strain of duck, its feeding and general environment, it will be ready for slaughter from around 56 days onwards, but the more access they have to free-range, the longer the growing period until slaughter weight. One of the best indications is to keep a close eye on the plumage. After becoming fully feathered, the ducklings will subsequently undergo a juvenile moult. Leaving slaughter until after this stage means that new feather stubs are present in the carcase, and these are often difficult to remove. Observing when a few neck feathers are shed is a good indication of when slaughtering should take place.

Before the birds are killed, food should be withheld for six hours, although access to drinking water should continue. They should be separated into small groups by means of moveable panels so that they can be caught without causing panic and stress. Catch a duck by its neck but do not lift it in this way. Slip one hand under the body to support it, while the other is placed on the back to confine the wings. (See photo on page 67). It will depend on the individual producer, as to whether slaughtering and processing take place on or off the site. Professional advice should be sought, and an excellent source of information is the *Humane Slaughter Association*. Another essential guide is *The Code of Practice for On-Farm Slaughter and Marketing of Poultry* available from DEFRA.

Eviscerating uses a similar technique as that used for gutting chickens. Cut off the head and suspend the carcase so that it can bleed into a bucket. Use poultry secateurs to snip off the neck, but retain the flap of skin. Make the hole at the neck end bigger and draw out the lungs. Then, make an incision around the vent, taking care not to puncture the intestines. Draw out the guts, then arrange the carcase neatly with the flap of skin folded over at the neck end. The neck, heart and gizzard can be retained for making stock, if required. Remember that food safety regulations apply for on-site processing. Consult the local Environmental Health Department for advice.

Plucking

Hand plucking is a time-consuming occupation, but small-scale machine pluckers and wax finishers are available from specialist suppliers. (See Reference section). The ducks are dry plucked and then wax is used to remove any remaining down or pin feathers. Where they are hand plucked, they are often singed briefly to achieve this. Wet plucking is also feasible. Here, is a letter that I received from Worcestershire, after a reader of *Country Smallholding* had asked for information:

"I scald a newly killed duck in hot water at 79-80⁰C with washing soda at the rate of (½oz) per gallon, for 90 seconds. When initially dunked, I rub the body with a spoon to work in the solution and agitate the bird in the water for the whole time. Rubber gloves are needed so you don't scald yourself - and beware - washing soda attacks aluminium (use stainless steel). The plucking takes about 15 minutes a bird. No, they don't taste funny! This method works with ducks and the Muscovy."

(Dave Allen, Worcestershire, *Country Smallholding*, January 2000)

Showing

All who keep ducks do not look upon them purely as layers of eggs or as table meat. Many like to exhibit them.
(Reginald Appleyard)

We are fortunate in Britain in having a national waterfowl show. Called the BWA Champion Waterfowl Exhibition, it takes place annually and offers an opportunity to see the very best of the domestic breeds on display. There are also waterfowl classes in many poultry and agricultural shows, both local and national.

Waterfowl classes are organised under the combined auspices of the British Waterfowl Association and the individual breed societies. Standards of excellence have been drawn up for each breed and are to be seen in the publication *BWA Standards*, as well as the Poultry Club of Great Britain's *Poultry Standards*. In America, the equivalent publication is the *American Standard of Perfection*, published by the American Poultry Association.

Only recognised domestic breeds are shown in waterfowl classes, although there may be some that come into the category of 'other breeds' because they are in insufficient numbers to have been standardized. For example, the Shetland, a small breed with similar markings to the Blue Swedish, is recognised but not yet standardized at the time of writing.

The first essential for the prospective exhibitor is to opt for a particular breed, join the breed society and obtain a copy of the relevant standards. The next step is to acquire some good breeding stock. This may not be as simple as it sounds for there may be a shortage or a waiting list for some breeds. The breed society will be able to help with information, while the BWA Yearbook also includes a breeders' list. See also the Breeders' Directory in *Country Smallholding* magazine.

Breeding stock obviously needs to be in the best of health and should be leg-ringed for identification. Good hatching records should be kept, followed by a record of development of the young birds, so that the best of a particular hatch can be selected for potential showing.

Talking to breeders and going to see waterfowl shows and exhibits is an excellent

These Indian Runners are part of a sheep dog trial demonstration at the Three Counties Showground, Malvern. The Runners take the place normally occupied by sheep. Note the plastic netting which makes a useful temporary pen.

Ducks on show at the Royal Showground, Stoneleigh.

preparation. Once you are ready to start exhibiting your own birds, send off to the show secretary of the particular show, in order to obtain a show schedule. This will give all the various classes that there are available, and the various conditions and dates. (There are also Junior categories). Decide on the classes to be entered, send off the application form and fee to the secretary and then concentrate on the ducks.

Select the very best ones for the particular category. Before the show, ensure that they are well, clean and looking their best. Practise putting them in and taking them out of show cages so that they are used to it. Their feet and webs may need a clean to remove any traces of mud before setting off.

Transporting the ducks in comfort is obviously an important aspect. Carrying cages that double up as show pens are available, as well as other purpose-made plastic or wooden pens. Pet carriers of the type that have barred sides for ventilation are also suitable. If large cardboard boxes are used, they should have plenty of holes made in the sides for there to be an adequate airflow. Once in the vehicle, the transport carrier should be well secured so that it does not move about in transit. Ducks will cope well with a short journey, but for longer distances, a stop in order to give them food and water will be necessary.

Once at the venue, report your arrival so that the paperwork can be completed, then place the ducks in their allocated pens. There are normally pens available, but it is vital to have checked this beforehand. Having good pens is vital if the ducks are to show themselves off properly. This includes having backing on them so that Indian Runners, for example, will be seen at their best. They are unlikely to stand properly unless a pen has backing. Ensure that the ducks have access to a drinker, then stand back and wait for the judging. You may be lucky. If not, there's always next time!

Health

Pekin drake
(F. Sewell, 1902)

And who so happy - oh who, as the duck and the kangaroo?
(Edward Lear, 1870)

There are fewer diseases affecting ducks than there are those troubling chickens, and the breeds of the northern hemisphere are hardier and more able to withstand the cold. There are some conditions which can affect them, however, and the main factors that prevent problems are as follows:

- Buy healthy stock in the first place.
- Quarantine new stock for at least 10 days before allowing them to join other ducks.
- Ideally, keep different ages separate (not always possible on a small scale).
- Provide housing that is dry, clean, wind-proof but well-ventilated.
- Provide and replenish clean, dry floor and nest litter regularly.
- Change swimming water frequently.
- Ideally, feed dry proprietary pellets and grain only, and avoid anything mouldy.
- Provide fresh drinking water every day.
- Clean feeders and drinkers regularly.
- Take measures to get rid of rats that carry disease.
- Avoid over-stocking and provide plenty of room, both indoors and outside.
- Rotate grassland on a seasonal basis.
- Always put young ducklings out on land previously unused by other birds.
- Get to know the ducks and watch out for unusual behaviour.

Suspicious signs to look out for include the following:

- Definite symptoms, eg, eye, nasal or vent discharge, lack of coordination.
- Limping or other unusual walk or stance.
- Lethargy, eg, staying sitting for a long period or a reluctance to go into the water.
- Lack of appetite (or excessive appetite).
- Excessive thirst.
- Thinness (breastbone feels sharp).
- General loss of condition, eg, scraggy feathers with lack of sheen.

Despite all precautions, a problem may arise and the following diseases are those that can affect ducks. Be aware, however, that small-scale, non-intensive enterprises are far less likely to have problems if the optimum conditions outlined above are provided. If a duck should display unusual symptoms, isolate it from the others in a small, protected pen, in case it is harbouring something infectious. Give fresh water and some dry proprietary pellets only and observe it. The chances are that it will recover. A little cider vinegar in the drinking water may be beneficial. Plain, live yoghurt has probiotic features, and is also useful after an antibiotic course, to help reinstate the normal gut organisms. Where a condition is affecting several birds, it is vital to get veterinary advice quickly. There are some conditions that are notifiable; in other words, the law requires that a vet or DEFRA be notified.

Aflatoxin poisoning Aflatoxins are produced by the moulds *Aspergillus flavus* and *A. parasiticus*. These are found on cereals and other foodstuffs that have not been stored properly, or have been stored too long and are damp. (Mouldy bread may also harbour these moulds). Ducks are particularly susceptible to aflatoxins, with even a small amount causing death. Be especially careful in feeding stale bread.

Aspergillosis (Fungal pneumonia) *Aspergillus fumigatus* fungus is the cause of this. It is found in mouldy litter, hay or feed. When spores are inhaled, the fungus grows in the lungs. Young birds are particularly at risk. Poor hatchery and brooder conditions can cause it, hence the common name of 'brooder pneumonia'. Humans can also be affected, as indicated by

Ducks can become quite tame. Regular observation makes it easier to spot problems.

its other common name of 'farmer's lung'. Symptoms are gasping and rapid breathing. Anti-fungal treatments are available but expensive. Prevention is best.

Avian influenza Caused by a myxovirus, this influenza is carried by airborne particles from the respiratory tract, as well as by droppings or people carrying it on their clothes or equipment. There are several different strains, and common symptoms include discharge from the nostrils or swollen head and neck in more virulent strains. Most birds recover from it, having then developed an immunity. Where it is followed by sinusitis, which is caused by a bacterium, an antibiotic from the vet will help to clear it, although in old birds the condition may become chronic.

Avian tuberculosis This is caused by the bacterium *Mycobacterium tuberculosis avium*, and is more common in older birds. It can take a long time to develop and is marked by lethargy and thinness. It is normally passed on via the droppings, so it is important to have clean litter. It can also be introduced by wild birds. If it has appeared on a site, it is possible to have the remaining ducks tested. Those that are free of the disease can then be moved to new housing and land.

Botulism (Limber neck) The source of this is the bacterium *Clostridium botulinum*, although it is not the organism itself that is the problem, but rather the toxins that it produces. Stagnant water with decaying material (dead animals) is the usual culprit, which is why it is so important to have only clean, well-aerated water for the ducks to swim and dabble in. Symptoms include weakness and lack of coordination, including drooping of the wings, eyelids and neck, eventually leading to paralysis and death. An anti-toxin is available, but this is only effective in mild cases. Prevention is best.

Coccidiosis There are a number of *Coccidia* protozoans that affect the intestines and are passed in droppings. They are specific to the various poultry. Ducks are less vulnerable than chickens, but can still become infected if they are on dirty litter or overused pasture. Ducklings are more at risk than adults so should always be given access to ground previously unused. If very young ones become infected, there may be no visible signs before death. Symptoms in older ones include a hunched-up stance, blood-stained diarrhoea and an inability to stand properly. Early veterinary diagnosis is important so that the appropriate anticoccidial preparation can be administered. The feeding of chick starter ration which contains an anticoccidiostat for them, is not recommended. A duck starter ration is preferable.

Colibacillosis The bacterium *Escherichia coli* is reponsible for a range of diseases that can affect the different age groups. In hatching eggs, it can cause infection of the yolk sac (omphalitis), which is why egg washing and incubator hygiene are so important. Septicaemia and peritonitis are conditions that can affect the birds if they have absorbed the bacterium. Again, good management of the environment is essential, particularly in periods of hot weather when infections are more common. Affected birds are listless and will refuse to eat, although they do drink. An antibiotic in the drinking water is the best treatment, followed by a move to fresh ground.

Duck viral hepatitis This is a highly contagious disease that affects young duck-lings. They are most at risk during the first four weeks of life when the disease is usually fatal. Older birds develop a resistance to it. Symptoms include paddling of the legs and arching the head and neck backwards. Prevention is the best approach, avoiding mixing different age groups too early. Breeders can be vaccinated against it so that immunity is passed on.

Duck viral enteritis (DVE, Duck plague) Characterised by weakness, diarrhoea, extreme thirst and a lack of coordination, this is a highly contagious disease with high mortality. It is caused by a herpes virus that is usually transmitted via the droppings or during mating. It is usually found in older birds, although it has also been found in ducklings. The droppings are often blood-stained, and blood may also be seen coming from the bill for haemorrhaging is associated with the condition. Ducks can now be innoculated against it. Breeding birds that are innoculated will pass on immunity to the young.

Egg binding Occasionally a laying duck may have a particularly large egg that she is not able to lay, and it becomes stuck. She may go backwards and forwards to the nest, to no avail, and may have a 'legs apart' walk. Apply *Vaseline* around the rim of the vent, and if possible hold her above a source of steam that bathes and relaxes the muscles. (How hot it is on your hands will indicate the degree of closeness). Hopefully, the egg will then be passed. If not, and the egg can be seen in the vent, piercing it from the outside and then 'hoiking' out the pieces has been known to work, as long as no pieces are left inside. This last option should only be undertaken when there is no hope otherwise. (If not removed the bird will die). An antibiotic is essential to combat infection.

External parasites Blood-sucking Northern mite and Red mite are external parasites that may affect ducks. The former is usually found on the head and neck. The latter, which is more rare on ducks, often lives in cracks in the house, emerging at night to feed off the ducks, then leaving them again. Lice may occasionally be a problem. These live off the scales of the skin and base of the feathers. A pyrethrum based powder can be applied to the plumage, with the application being repeated a week later. Treat the house in the same way. Keep the birds off the pond for a day, not only to give the powder a chance to work, but also because it is toxic to fish. A herbal preparation such as *Barrier* is effective against both mites and lice.

Feather pecking If ducks are pecking their own feathers or those of others, check for external parasites and treat as above. In artificially reared ducklings it is important that they do not get wet before they are able to preen and waterproof their feathers, otherwise the plumage forms 'spikes' that attract attention. Ensure that the ducks are getting a balanced diet in case the behaviour is an attempt to make up for a deficiency in the food intake. If it is a manifestation of bullying, separate the bully from the others, until the behaviour stops. Provide enough space to prevent boredom. Hang up some greens in the run to provide interest.

Impaction (Crop binding) This is a blockage of the digestive tract in the crop area. The crop is not as well-defined as that of a chicken, but is a slightly wider section of the tract. Coarse or stalky material is usually the cause, so exclude these from the diet and always provide grit. Where vegetables are given loose (rather than suspended in a bunch) ensure that they are chopped into small pieces. An impaction can be treated by giving the duck a spoonful of cooking oil, and then kneading the crop area. Sour crop, where an acidic condition is causing problems, can be treated with Epsom salts.

Infectious serositis (New duck disease) Caused by the organism *Riemeralla anatipestifer*, this disease has a high mortality rate, with symptoms including eye discharge, diarrhoea, lack of coordination, head shaking and twisting of the neck. Birds may also be found on their backs, paddling their legs. There is a vaccine that provides protection, while antibiotics are effective in dealing with outbreaks in unprotected flocks.

Internal parasites Internal worms can affect ducks, although older birds are able to tolerate a certain level of infestation. Thin birds with ruffled, 'staring' plumage may have a heavy burden of parasites. Many duck keepers worm their birds once a year, as a matter of course. *Flubenvet* powder can be mixed in with the food and administered over a period of a week.

Lameness Lameness as a result of leg strains can result from having to negotiate awkward surfaces so it is important to provide ramps for ease of movement. Callouses on the underside of the webs can also be a problem in these conditions. The latter may need to be lanced if the pus has been covered by a thick skin. Staphylocci infections in the legs and feet can also cause limping. Here, there may be swelling and the infected area feels hot to the touch. An antibiotic treatment is effective. Non-indigenous ornamentals must be given frost-protection in winter, to avoid foot frostbite.

Newcastle disease (Fowl pest) This is a notifiable disease and where it occurs, the affected flock is slaughtered, while all movement of poultry is suspended in the area. It causes respiratory and digestive problems, and high mortality. There is a vaccine available that offers protection against it.

Pasteurellosis (Fowl cholera) The bacterium *Pasteurella multocida* is spread by wild birds and rats. It causes respiratory infection and diarrhoea that is watery and greenish. Antibiotics are effective.

Poisoning Poisons that affect ducks include: poorly placed rat poison; lead from fishing and shooting activities, as well as some paints; antifreeze (ethylene glycol) and car oils left lying around; some insecticides; phosphorus from spent fireworks; salt from excess of kitchen scraps.

One of the author's Muscovy drakes which developed a slipped wing. Efforts to bind up the wing were to no avail, but he was kept as a pet, although not allowed to breed. Here he is moulting.

Toxic plants are not normally taken by well-fed ducks, but there is always a risk. It is best to avoid the following in the areas to which they have access: lily of the valley, deadly nightshade, hemlock, laburnum, 'green' potatoes and foxgloves.

Prolapse A heavy layer may suffer from a prolapse, where the end of the oviduct protrudes and turns outwards. Similarly, the penis of the drake may not retract. If the conditions do not improve of their own accord, there is nothing that can be done. In both cases culling is advisable on humanitarian grounds.

Salmonellosis There are many salmonella organisms that cause disease. Wild birds and rats carry them, while droppings and dirty conditions also encourage them. Some strains, such as *Salmonella enteriditis*, can pass directly from the parent bird to the young, via the egg. Breeder birds can be tested to ascertain this.

Paratyphoid is caused by *Salmonella typhimurium*, and can affect all ages. A hunched-up stance is symptomatic of disease, along with watery, cream-coloured diarrhoea, great thirst but poor appetite. Antibiotics are effective, but birds that recover may suffer from arthritic conditions. Provide clean conditions and avoid it.

Slipped wing (Angel wing) Heavy breeds or birds that have been fed too high a protein ration in their formative period, may suffer from a slipped wing, where the wing droops down. Sometimes it may protrude sideways, a condition referred to as 'angel wing'. In its early stages, it is worth trying binding the wing in place.

Watery eye (Sticky eye) A continually running eye is usually the result of an infection. There may also be white patches. It is more common where there is a lack of clean, aerated water for the duck to dip its head in. An antibiotic preparation is effective. The condition may also be related to a vitamin A deficiency. Ensure that a balanced ration is made available.

Wet feather Reference has already been made to the fact that artificially-reared ducklings should be kept out of water until their preening glands are functioning. Occasionally, one comes across one that does not seem to achieve this. Make sure the diet is adequate, with no deficiencies. Konrad Lorenz, the great waterfowl expert, claimed that rubbing the bird with a piece of silk emulated the action of the mother bird and this encouraged self-preening.

Reference section

Appendix I: Daily and Seasonal Care

Daily

- Check that run/enclosure/aviary door is secure then open the house door.
- Good morning ducks!
- Provide compound feed such as pellets in a clean, heavy-based feeder. Some ornamentals may require floating pellets on water.
- Observe birds for any signs of illness, limping, etc, while they are feeding.
- Check drinkers and refill as necessary.
- Collect eggs. Check later for any late-laid eggs.
- Check nest boxes and floor, and replace litter as necessary.
- Give grain feed in the afternoon.
- Check condition of pond or dabbling water supply.
- Ensure that all ducks are in during the evening. Good night ducks!

Periodically

- Clean out and refill pond as necessary. Check other water courses and carry out any repairs, as required.
- Move any small moveable houses as required.
- Check for signs of vermin such as rats and take appropriate action.
- Check pasture or exercise area for signs of wear. Use new area as necessary. Lime old area and leave fallow to recover. If necessary, re-sow grass.
- Clean out aviary.
- Check fencing for signs of weakness or burrowing under.
- Check electric fencing current. Strim grass that might otherwise 'short' current.
- Mow or strim pasture to make new, short grasses available for grazing ducks.

Spring and Summer

- Ensure that nesting boxes and nesting areas are prepared.
- Prepare housing for broody hens, if to be used.
- Check incubator if to be used.
- Check brooder, if to be used.
- Watch out for corvids stealing eggs.
- Buy table ducklings for rearing.
- Buy ducklings or young ducks for future breeding.
- Observe performance of egg producers and keep production records.
- Watch out for mites on young birds that have not yet been on water.

Autumn and Winter

- Take action against predators and vermin.
- Watch out for signs of internal worms. If necessary give a vermifuge in the feed.
- Select future breeding stock as they come into their nuptial plumage (also based on production records, good examples of the standards and good health).
- Buy (or sell) birds as breeding stock.
- Select birds for their future show-winning potential. Send off for show schedules.
- Ensure that water supplies are kept free of ice.
- Lime pasture areas that are to be left fallow.
- Prune trees and shrubs in enclosures or aviary. Ensure that sufficient perching areas are available for perching ducks.
- Watch out for two-legged thieves!

Appendix II: **Ducks miscellany**

Expressions

To duck - to move the head down sharply in order to avoid being struck.
To duck out - to make a quick exit or take evasive action.
Ducking and diving - taking evasive action.
Out for a duck - dismissed from a game of cricket without having scored.
Breaking a duck - scoring a first run of the innings.
Ducker - old name for one who was in charge of ducks or of a wild duck decoy.
Lame duck - old Stock Exchange expression for one who could not pay his losses.
Waddle out of the alley - action of lame duck not allowed to return until debts paid.
Duck legs - short legs.
D.A. (duck's arse) haircut - hair shaped like a duck's tail at the back of the head.
Duck walk - a waddling way of walking.
Duck's meat - old name for pond duck weed.
Duck egg colour - a pale blue-green colour.
Duckie (Ducky) - term of endearment: from *dukke*, Danish/Shetland name for a girl.
Duck dub - old name for a duck pond.
Duck landing craft - from the officially designated military DUKW craft.
Duck pin - short bowling pin.
Duck soup - an easy task.
Duck boards - path of wooden slats over mud or in trench.
Duck hawk - peregrine or marsh harrier.
Duck material - strong linen or cotton fabric for small sails or sailor's clothing.
Ducking stool - chair at end of pole for immersing scolds to teach them a lesson.
Widdles (or waddles) - old names for ducklings.
Dilly dilly - old way of calling ducks.
Dilly dally - waste time
Like a dying duck in a thunderstorm - flabbergasted.
Like water off a duck's back - not affected at all.
Like a duck to water - very readily.
Quack - medical charlatan with quack remedies.
Quack quack - childish name for duck. Also an expression of its call.

Duck games

Duck - where a stone is placed on a larger one and attempts are then made to dislodge it by throwing a stone at it from an agreed distance.

Ducks and drakes - where flat stones are thrown on water at an angle, in order to make them skim and strike the water several times before sinking. In the past, the following rhyme was said, and unless the stone rose at the end of each line, the manouvre had to be repeated. Three unsuccessful attempts meant that the game was lost: *"Hen-pen, duck and mallard. Amen"*.

Duck anecdotes

Dancing duck. In the 1920s my father was in Shanghai when he came across a street stall advertising a 'dancing duck'. Sure enough, the duck began to dance, raising one foot and then the other when its owner began to play on a penny whistle. At first impressed, my father soon discovered the secret of the dancing duck. It was standing on a metal plate under which the owner had placed lighted candles!

Wing hearth brush - When I was a child in Wales, the wings from table ducks or geese were usually saved so that they could be used as hearth brushes. The wing tips were just right for getting into small crevices but it didn't do to singe the feathers for the smell was overpowering.

Famous ducks. Donald Duck - Walt Disney. The Ugly Duckling - Hans Christian Anderson

Further information

Bibliography

British Waterfowl Standards. C. & M. Ashton. B.W.A. 1999
British Poultry Standards. V. Roberts. Blackwell. 1997
Rerum Rusticarum. Varro.
Ducks. R. Appleyard. Poultry World. 1949
Ducks and Duck Breeding. C.S. Roscoe. Crowther. 1941
Ducks and Geese at Home. Roberts. 1991
Domestic Ducks and Geese. F. Hams. Shire. 2000
Ducks and Geese in your Backyard. R. & G. Luttmann. Rodale. 1978
Domesticated Ducks and Geese. J. Batty. Spur. 1979
The Domestic Duck. C. & M. Ashton. Crowood. 2001.
Races of Domestic Poultry. E. Brown.
The New Duck Handbook. H.S. Raethel. Barrons. 1989
Storey's Guide to Raising Ducks. D. Holderread. Storey. 2001.
The World of Wildfowl. E. Jackson & M. Ogilvie. The Wildfowl Trust/ Macmillan. 1973
Wildfowl at Home. A. Birkbeck. Roberts. 1991
Manual of Waterfowl Management. S. Tarsnane. BWA. 1982
Practical Slaughter of Poultry. HSA. 1995
Codes of Recommendations for the Welfare of Livestock: Ducks. DEFRA. 1999
Brown Rats. C. Matheson. S.T publications. 1962
The Illustrated Book of Poultry. Lewis Wright. Cassell. 1874

Organisations

The British Waterfowl Association. Rachel Boer, Oaklands, Blind Lane, Tamworth in Arden, Solihull B94 5HS Tel/Fax: 01564 741821. www.waterfowl.org.uk
Domestic Waterfowl Club. Limetree Cottages, Brightwalton, Newbury, Berks RG20 7BZ Tel: 01488 638014
Poultry Club of Great Britain. Mike Clark, 30 Grosvenor Road, Frampton, Boston, Lincs PE20 1DB www.poultryclub.org
The Scottish Waterfowl Club. S.W. Simister, Kirkpatrick Hill, Closeburn, Thornhill, Dumfriesshire Tel: 01848 331696
British Call Duck Club. Maes y Coed, Llanarth, Ceredigion SA47 0RG Tel: 01545 580425
Call Duck Association. Graham Barnard, Ty Cymdar, Cwrt y Cadno, Llanwrda, Carmarthenshire SA19 8YH Tel: 01558 650532
Indian Runner Duck Association. Julian Burrell, Coombe Cottages, Lamellion, Liskeard, Cornwall PL14 4JU Tel: 01579 340557
Runner Duck Club. Des Little, Penfeidr, Crinow, Narbeth, Dyfed SA67 8TB Tel: 01834 861003

Suppliers

Stock

When buying pure-bred ducks, make sure that they come from a reputable stockist. There is not room to list individual breeders here but *Country Smallholding* magazine has an excellent *Breeders' Directory* in every issue. It is also listed on their website at www.countrysmallholding.com
The *British Waterfowl Association* also produce a breeders' list. (See address under *Organisations*).
Commercial layers (Khaki Campbells) can be obtained from *Kortlangs Duck Farm.* Ashford, Kent. Tel: 01233 623431.
Commercial meat birds can be obtained from *Cherry Valley Farms Ltd.* Rothwell, Market Rasen, Lincs LN7 6BJ. Tel: 01472 371271. www.cherryvalley.co.uk

Housing

The Domestic Fowl Trust. Honeybourne, Nr. Evesham, Worcs WR11 5QG Tel: 01386 833083 www.mywebpage.net/domestic-fowl-trust
Forsham Cottage Arks. Goreside Farm, Great Chart, Ashford, Kent TN26 1JU Tel: 01233 820229 www.forshamcottagearks.co.uk
Gardencraft. Tremadog, Porthmadog, Gwynedd, LL49 9RC Tel: 01766 513036
Littleacre Products. Botley House, School Lane, Hints, Tamworth B78 3DW Tel: 01543 481312
Lifestyles UK Ltd. Lakeside Court, Upton Warren, Bromsgrove, Worcs B61 7EY Tel: 01527 880078
Smiths Sectional Buildings. Unit 12, Barton Ct, 63 Hyde Rd, Chilwell, Notts NG9 4AJ Tel: 0115 939 0654

Incubators

Aliwal Incubators. Hilltop Farm, Tacolneston, Norwich, Norfolk NR16 1BP Tel/Fax: 01508 489328
Brinsea Products. Station Rd, Sandford, N. Somerset BS25 5RA Tel: 01934 830930 www.brinsea.co.uk
Curfew Incubators. (SARL). Tel: 01621 741923. www.curfewincubators.com
Interhatch. 27 Derbyshire Lane, Sheffield S8 9EA Tel: 0700 462 8228
MS Incubators. Stoneybroke Cottage, Bruntingthorpe Rd, Peatling Parva, LE17 5RB Tel: 01116 247 8335
Natureform Hatchery Systems. P.O. Box 641, Harrow HA3 7US Tel: 01608 686591. www.natureform.com
Southern Aviaries. Tinkers Lane, Hadlow Down, Uckfield TN22 4EU Tel: 01825 830930

Pond Equipment

Aquaplancton. Clavering Cote, Little London, Stowmarket, Suffolk IP14 2ES. Tel: 01449 774532
Bradshaws. Nicholson Link, Clifton Moor, York YO1 1SS Tel: 01904 691169 - Liners
Cyprio Ltd. Hards Road, Frognall, Peterborough PE6 8RR Tel: 01778 344502 - Pumps, etc
Fawcetts Liners. Back Lane, Longton PR4 5JA Tel: 01772 612125
Lotus Water Garden Products. PO Box 36, Junction St, Burnley, Lancs BB12 0NA Tel: 01282 420771
Midland Butyl. Freepost 288, Ripley, Derby DE5 9BR Tel: 01773 748169 - Liners
H.D. Sharman Ltd. High Peak Works, Chapel-en -le-Frith, Stockport, Cheshire SK12 6HW Tel: 01298 812371/2 - Liners
Tuck Plastics. Units F & G, Conduit Lane Indus. Estate, Hoddesdon, Herts Tel/Fax: 01992 443489 - Liners
T.P. Activity Toys Ltd (Paddling pools) Severn Rd, Stourport-on-Severn, Worcs DY13 9EX. Tel: 01299 827728

Duck Feeds

Allen and Page. Norfolk Mill, Shipdham, Thetford, Norfolk IP25 7SD Tel: 01362 822900 www.smallholderfeed.co.uk
BOCM Pauls Ltd. P.O. Box 2, Olympia Mills, Barlby Road, Selby, Yorks YO8 5AF Tel: 01757 244000
Clark and Butcher Ltd. Lion Mills, Soham, Ely, Cambs CB7 5HY Tel: 01353 720237
Mazuri Zoo Foods. P.O. Box 705, Witham, Essex CM8 3AD Tel: 01376 511260
W.H.Marriage and Sons Ltd. Chelmer Mill, New Street, Chelmsford, Essex CM1 1PN Tel: 01245 612000/ 354455. www.marriagefeeds.co.uk

Electric Fencing

Electranets Ltd. 31 Westfield Avenue, Brockworth, Gloucester GL3 4AU Tel: 01452 617841
Electric Fencing Direct. Tel: 01732 833976
Hotline Renco Ltd. Tel: 01626 331188 www.hotline-fencing.co.uk
G.A. and M.J. Strange. Broadfield, North Wraxall, Chippenham, Wilts SN4 7AD Tel: 01225 891236

Pest Control

Acorn Pest Control. 18 Marshall Road, Exhall, Coventry CV7 9BX Tel: 02476 491689 www.acorn-pest-control.co.uk
Amtex. Unit 2, Amtex Building, Southern Avenue, Leominster, Herefordshire HR6 0QF Tel: 01568 610900 www.thezapper.co.uk
Phoenix. Tel: 01584 711701
Sorex Ltd. Widnes, Cheshire WA8 8TJ Tel: 0151 420 7151

General and Equipment Suppliers

Ascott Smallholding Supplies. Dudleston Hth, Ellesmere SY12 9LJ Tel: 0845 130 6285 www.ascottshop.com
Cyril Bason (Stokesay) Ltd. Bankhouse, Corvedale Rd, Craven Arms, Shropshire SY7 9NG Tel: 01588 673204/673242.
Danro Ltd. Unit 68, Jaydon Industrial Estate, Station Road, Earl Shilton, Leicester LE9 7GA Tel: 01455 847061/2. (Egg cartons and labels). www.danroltd.co.uk
The Domestic Fowl Trust - see Housing
Oxmoor Smallholder Supplies. Harlthorpe, East Yorkshire YO8 6DW Tel: 01757 288186
Parkland Products, Stone-in-Oxney, Tenterden, Kent TN30 7JT. (Auto feeders) www.parklandproducts.co.uk
Pintail Sporting Services Ltd. Tel: 01794 524472
Solway Feeders Ltd. Dundrennan, Kirkcudbright, Scotland DG6 4QH Tel: 01557 500253 www.solwayfeeders.com
SPR. Greenfields Farm, Eastergate, Chichester, Sussex PO20 6RU Tel: 01243 542815
Woodside Poultry and Livestock Centre. Woodside Rd, Slip End Village, Nr. Luton, Beds LU1 4DG Tel: 01582 841044 www.woodsidefarm.co.uk

Index